Human Resource Management in an Emerging South Asian Economy

This book focuses on human resource management (HRM) in the country context of Brunei Darussalam, analysing, comparing and contrasting domestic enterprises (DEs) with multinational enterprises (MNEs), and oil and gas with non-oil and -gas sectors, and draws out the comparative lessons for understanding the potential and performance consequences of HR interventions in resource-centred national economies. Work carried out more recently drawing a contrast between Asian capitalisms has established a number of important defining aspects inherent in economies in Asia; this helps to present approaches to establishing the way in which Brunei may be seen to be aligned with, and depart from, other business systems and frameworks in Asia.

The existing literature highlights a trend towards focusing on the Asian context; however, most studies have focused on specific Asian countries, and research conducted in other contexts remains scarce. As the region gains economic prosperity, it is increasingly important to conduct some work that will be able to highlight the relevant HRM system(s) for other Asian contexts. Although some emerging Asian economies are still quite far from achieving developed nation status, it is however essential to understand the HRM systems prevalent in such economies as they can contribute greatly to the economic development there. Hence, this book highlights the importance of viewing the development and nature of HR in Brunei and locates the practice of HRM within the wider economic and political context, and draws out the theoretical and practical implications for understanding continuity in change in HR practice, and similarities with and differences from other emerging markets. It will be of interest to researchers, academics, and students in international and comparative human resource management.

Tamer K Darwish is a Reader in Human Resource Management (HRM), and the Head of HRM Research Centre in the Business School, University of Gloucestershire.

Pengiran Muda Abdul Fattaah is the Chairman of Baiduri Bank, Brunei.

Routledge Studies in Human Resource Development
Edited by Monica Lee, Lancaster University, UK

HRD theory is changing rapidly. Recent advances in theory and practice, how we conceive of organisations and of the world of knowledge, have led to the need to reinterpret the field. This series aims to reflect and foster the development of HRD as an emergent discipline.

Encompassing a range of different international, organisational, methodological and theoretical perspectives, the series promotes theoretical controversy and reflective practice.

26 **Identity as a Foundation for Human Resource Development**
 Edited by Kate Black, Russell Warhurst and Sandra Corlett

27 **Positive Ageing and Human Resource Development**
 Edited by Diane Keeble-Ramsay and Andrew Armitage

28 **Work, Working and Work Relationships in a Changing World**
 Edited by Clare Kelliher and Julia Richardson

29 **Human Resource Management in an Emerging
 South Asian Economy**
 The Case of Brunei
 Edited by Tamer K Darwish and Pengiran Muda Abdul Fattaah

Also published in the series in paperback:

Action Research in Organisations
Jean McNiff, accompanied by Jack Whitehead

Understanding Human Resource Development
A research-based approach
Edited by Jim Stewart, Jim McGoldrick, and Sandra Watson

For more information about this series, please visit: https://www.routledge.com

Human Resource Management in an Emerging South Asian Economy

The Case of Brunei

Edited by
Tamer K Darwish and
Pengiran Muda Abdul Fattaah

Routledge
Taylor & Francis Group

LONDON AND NEW YORK

Library of Congress Cataloging-in-Publication Data
Names: Darwish, Tamer K, editor. | Fattaah, Pengiran Muda
Abdul, editor.
Title: Human resource management in an emerging South Asian
economy : the case of Brunei / edited by Tamer K Darwish and
Pengiran Muda Abdul Fattaah.
Description: New York : Routledge, 2020. |
Series: Routledge studies in human resource development |
Includes bibliographical references and index.
Identifiers: LCCN 2019049945 | ISBN 9780367142636
(hardback) | ISBN 9780429030963 (ebook)
Subjects: LCSH: Personnel management—Brunei. | Personnel
management—South Asia. | Entrepreneurship—Brunei. |
Entrepreneurship—South Asia.
Classification: LCC HF5549.2.S62 H86 2020 |
DDC 658.300954—dc23
LC record available at https://lccn.loc.gov/2019049945

ISBN: 978-0-367-14263-6 (hbk)
ISBN: 978-1-03-217529-4 (pbk)
DOI: 10.4324/9780429030963

Typeset in Sabon
by codeMantra

To my parents, HRH Prince Mohamed Bolkiah and HRH Pengiran Anak Isteri Pengiran Anak Zariah

To the loving memory of Professor Khalil Darwish

To our families and friends

Contents

1 Introduction   1
TAMER K DARWISH AND PENGIRAN MUDA ABDUL FATTAAH

2 The Context of Brunei Darussalam   7
PENGIRAN MUDA ABDUL FATTAAH AND TAMER K DARWISH

3 Comparative Human Resource Management   21
CHRIS BREWSTER AND WASHIKA HAAK-SAHEEM

4 International Human Resource Management   37
PENGIRAN MUDA ABDUL FATTAAH, WASHIKA HAAK-SAHEEM,
CHRIS BREWSTER AND TAMER K DARWISH

5 Institutions, Complementarity, Human Resource
Management, and Performance   52
SATWINDER SINGH, TAMER K DARWISH, GEOFFREY WOOD,
AND PENGIRAN MUDA ABDUL FATTAAH

6 Resource Cursed Economies and HR Practices   75
TAMER K DARWISH, PENGIRAN MUDA ABDUL FATTAAH,
GEOFFREY WOOD, AND SATWINDER SINGH

7 The Role of HR Directors in Multinational and
Domestic Enterprises   88
SATWINDER SINGH, GEOFFREY WOOD, TAMER K DARWISH,
JOCELYNE FLEMING, AND PENGIRAN MUDA ABDUL FATTAAH

8 Recruitment, Training, and Retention Practices:
Do Domestic Firms Differ from Multinationals?   104
PENGIRAN MUDA ABDUL FATTAAH, SATWINDER SINGH,
AND TAMER K DARWISH

9 Performance Appraisals, Incentives, and Reward
Practices in Domestic Vs Multinational Enterprises 118
SATWINDER SINGH, PENGIRAN MUDA ABDUL FATTAAH,
AND TAMER K DARWISH

10 A Comparative Perspective on HRM in Brunei 131
GEOFFREY WOOD

List of Contributors 141
Index 145

1 Introduction

Tamer K Darwish and Pengiran Muda Abdul Fattaah

Overview

This book focuses on human resource management (HRM) in the country context of Brunei Darussalam; analyses, compares, and contrasts domestic enterprises (DEs) and multinational enterprises (MNEs), and oil and gas and non-oil and -gas sectors; and draws out the comparative lessons for understanding the potential and performance consequences of HR interventions in resource-centred national economies. In this book, we present a number of empirical works that have been carried out in the context of Brunei, where the oil and gas industry is recognised as being responsible for a large majority of the country's national income (Mohamed et al., 2013; Darwish et al., 2017; Singh et al., 2019). Nonetheless, one of the main goals underpinning Brunei's economic activities is that of diversification, with the country recognising that gas and oil are finite and that there is a need to overcome the resource curse (Auty, 1993; Singh et al., 2019). Work carried out more recently, drawing a contrast between Asian capitalisms, has established a number of important defining aspects inherent in economies in Asia; this helps to present approaches to establishing the way in which Brunei may be seen to be aligned with, and depart from, other business systems and frameworks in Asia (Witt & Redding, 2013, 2014; Fainshmidt et al., 2018; Singh et al., 2019).

In addition, there is the question of whether or not context, and the degree to which an organisation is embedded within it, has the potential to dominate formal business roles and structures so as to establish the degree to which an organisation implements strategic people management (Singh et al., 2019). A wide range of studies present the view that MNEs in particular face greater expectations to act as 'norm entrepreneurs', establishing and developing new practices that test and confront different ways of doing things (see Björkman & Lervik, 2007; Dore, 2008; Singh et al., 2019). This could potentially involve a greater number of innovative and strategic methods in regard to HRM (Brewster et al., 2008; Singh et al., 2019).

Empirical HRM studies, some of which have been conducted in the context of MNEs, have largely concentrated on comparing HRM practices in subsidiaries of MNEs in the context of developed nations (see, e.g., Guest & Hoque, 1996; Boxall et al., 2007). Research conducted on MNEs is often aimed at understanding how MNEs utilise expatriates in subsidiaries as well as the selection, training, and management of such employees (Dowling & Welch, 2004; Haak-Saheem & Brewster, 2017); these processes are often susceptible to the cultural traits of host nations (Gooderham & Brewster, 2003) and to the presence of societal context inherent in the host countries' social and economic institutions (Morishima, 1995), which can also notably affect the practices and processes adopted by companies. This book attempts to fill a gap in the existing literature by conducting and presenting empirical works along similar lines in a non-Western setting and in the context of an emerging South Asian economy where institutional arrangements are fluid and developing. Fluidity or institutional weakness at the national level would be counterbalanced through institutional solutions being implemented in such a way as to support and encourage particular practices at the organisational level, focused on overcoming common issues across specific industries or arenas (Singh et al., 2019). The present book presents several implications for theory and practice, both within the context in which the research was conducted more broadly.

Statement of Significance

It is important to highlight that most comparative work in international human resource management (IHRM) has been conducted in Western developed nations. For the growth and development of IHRM, it is essential to examine the relevance of HRM, which can assist in assessing the degree to which HRM has gained strategic importance in different parts of the world. Identifying the main factors and variables determining HRM in different settings will help in analysing the applicability of HRM approaches in different regions, as well as highlighting the context-specific nature of HRM practices (Guthrie & Olian, 1991; Jackson & Schuler, 1995; Budhwar & Debrah, 2001; Darwish et al., 2017; Singh et al., 2019).

The existing literature (Budhwar, 2004; Singh et al., 2019) highlights a trend towards focusing on the Asian context; however, most studies have focused on China or Japan, and research conducted in other contexts is scarce. As the region gains economic prosperity, it is increasingly important to conduct research that will be able to highlight the relevant HRM system(s) for other Asian contexts. Furthermore, although some emerging Asian economies are still quite far from achieving developed nation status, it is nevertheless essential to understand the HRM systems prevalent in these economies as they can contribute greatly to the economic development there (Tayeb, 1995; Debrah et al., 2000).

Hence, the present book explores various aspects of IHRM in the context of an emerging and as yet oil- and gas-rich state. Its significance arises from the fact that it deals with HR practices in the context of both DEs and MNEs operating in the country to elicit insights into the functioning of HR practices to draw lessons for both theory and practice, as well as for DEs and MNEs that might have a great deal to learn from each other. Further, it is worth noting that, within commodity-centred economies, there are likely to be significant differences in HRM practice between the mineral and non-mineral sectors; hence, it could be argued that the human dimension of competitiveness is likely to be accorded particular importance when it comes to the challenges facing the non-primary commodity-based sectors (Darwish et al., 2017). Therefore, the present book also looks at sectors when investigating HRM aspects, differentiating between oil and gas, and non-oil and non-gas.

Structure of the Book

After this introduction, the book is structured as follows:

Chapter 2 presents a profile of the country of Brunei Darussalam. It first presents an overview of Brunei's geographic and demographic structure, followed by an overview of the historical and legal background of the country. The chapter then explores the economic system presently prevailing in the country, as well as the rationale for selecting Brunei as a case study. Finally, it discusses the importance of HRM and its study in the country of Brunei.

Chapter 3 focuses on comparative HRM. It explores the differences between nations in the way that they manage their human resources. Within a context of increasing globalisation, the chapter highlights how context matters to HRM. Fundamental to understanding these differences between countries are two concepts: the notions of cultural and institutional differences, and the notions of convergence and divergence. The chapter contributes to a better understanding of the main concepts and theories relevant to comparative HRM. First, it shows that cultural and institutional explanations are valuable to the comparative HRM approach. Further, it argues that convergence of trends is apparent, but complete convergence remains unrealistic. Finally, it outlines some of the key theoretical, empirical, and practical challenges posed by a comparative approach to HRM.

Chapter 4 provides insights into the concepts and theories behind HRM and IHRM, as well as exploring the various concepts that may affect the ways HRM is utilised by MNEs and other forms of internationally operating firms. Additionally, it reviews and critically discusses the theoretical and empirical work that has been carried out to explain the differences between IHRM in domestic organisations and in MNEs, highlighting the importance of understanding these differences when looking at the relationship between HRM and performance. Given the increasing role of contextual factors in the field of HRM, the chapter addresses the relevance of the current international business environment within the development and execution of HRM practices and policies.

Chapter 5 presents research results on the rate and effect of various specific bundles of HR practices on organisational performance in Brunei. The literature available on the subject of comparative capitalism suggests that, across more developed societies, it is common for a mutually supportive nature to be identified in relation to informal and formal regulations, which are maintained through linked and well-considered HR systems, centred on enhancing organisational performance. On the other hand, in situations where there is a lack of robustness in institutional arrangements, comparable incentives for distributing mutually supporting HR bundles will be lacking. Whilst these bundles are adequate, they are not well positioned to achieve any improved results. This has essentially been the case in the instance of the petro-state of Brunei, with the adoption of comprehensive HR frameworks found to work no better than individual approaches.

Chapter 6 explores HR practices in resource-cursed economies, with a particular focus on the context of Brunei. The literature available on the resource curse implies that organisations in non-oil and -gas sectors across petro-states experience a number of key obstacles to achieving competitiveness and becoming self-sustaining. This chapter investigates the link between particular HR policies and practices and business performance; emphasis is placed on examining and drawing contrasts between oil and gas and non-oil and -gas sectors, whilst further seeking to highlight the comparative lessons aimed at garnering insight into the possible and performance-related results associated with HR interventions in resource-focused national economies.

Chapter 7 explores the comparative effect of context on the senior management role. A comparison is presented between HR directors of DEs and those working in MNEs in the case of a developing market setting, in the country context of Brunei. This chapter presents support for the perceived value of MNEs in establishing more innovative and combined methods for managing people, although there have remained a number of limitations in terms of the degree to which they might position themselves as evangelists in the case of new methods implemented by their local peers. On the other hand, local organisations are seen to be far more inclined to emphasise administrative considerations as opposed to strategic ones. The implications for theory and practice are drawn out in the chapter.

Chapter 8 explores the behavioural differences identifiable when considering the recruitment, training and retention methods, and approaches applied by DEs in comparison with MNEs in the context of Brunei. Following the literature survey, various propositions are devised and empirically tested, and it is concluded that MNEs apply greater rigour when progressing through the recruitment and training processes, whilst also ensuring meticulous approaches when completing promotion. This chapter provides further understanding of and insight into HR practices specific to two different organisational types, whilst also providing valuable recommendations and implications for future work.

Chapter 9 focuses on performance appraisals, incentives and rewards practices. Only a small volume of previous study has been directed towards comparative analysis of HRM practices across MNEs and DEs. The majority of such examination in this field has, rather, drawn contrasts between the HRM practices implemented by MNEs' subsidiaries, with most of it completed in relation to industrialised countries. Hence, this chapter presents an analysis from the context of Brunei, on the way in which HR practices, namely appraisals, incentives, and rewards, are delivered, explained, and monitored in the case of DEs in comparison with MNEs, as well as the similarities and differences between the two.

Finally, Chapter 10 explores the challenges and opportunities in Brunei and the wider region. There has been a growing body of work on HRM in a wide cross section of emerging markets. There was initially a strong focus on cross-cultural approaches that sought to explain both the dominance of specific types of practice in emerging markets and how local cultures conferred both challenges and opportunities. More recently, the focus has shifted to comparative institutional approaches, in both helping to explain the process of systemic development and change and enabling closer links to be drawn between HR practice and the wider political economy. This chapter locates the practice of HRM in Brunei within the wider political context and draws out the implications for understanding continuity in change in HR practice, and similarities with and differences from other emerging markets.

References

Auty, R. (1993). *Sustaining development in mineral economies: The resource curse thesis*. London: Routledge.

Björkman, I., & Lervik, J. E. (2007). Transferring HR practices within multinational corporations. *Human Resource Management Journal*, 17, 4, 320–335.

Boxall, P., Purcell, J., & Wright, P. (2007). *The Oxford handbook of human resource management*. New York: Oxford University Press.

Brewster, C., Wood, G., & Brookes, M. (2008). Similarity, isomorphism and duality? Recent survey evidence on the HRM policies of MNCs. *British Journal of Management*, 19, 4, 320–342.

Budhwar, P. (2004). *Managing human resources in Asia-Pacific*. London: Routledge.

Budhwar, P., & Debrah, Y. (2001). Rethinking comparative and cross national human resource management research. *International Journal of Human Resource Management*, 12, 3, 497–515.

Darwish, T., Mohamed, A. F., Wood, G., Singh, S., & Fleming, J. (2017). Can HRM alleviate the negative effects of the resource curse on firms? Evidence from Brunei. *Personnel Review*, 46, 8, 1931–1947.

Debrah, Y. A., McGovern, I., & Budhwar, P. (2000). Complementarity or competition: The development of human resources in a growth triangle. *International Journal of Human Resource Management*, 11, 314–335.

Dore, R. (2008). Best practice winning out? *Socio-Economic Review*, 6, 4, 779–784.

Dowling, P. J., & Welch, D. E. (2004). *International human resource management: Managing people in a multinational context* (4th edn). London: Thomson.

Fainshmidt, S., Judge, W. Q., Aguilera, R. V., & Smith, A. (2016). Varieties of institutional systems: A contextual taxonomy of understudied countries. *Journal of World Business*, 53, 3, 307–322.

Gooderham, P. N., & Brewster, C. (2003). Convergence, stasis or divergence? Personnel management in Europe. *Scandinavian Journal of Business Research*, 17, 1, 6–18.

Guest, D. E., & Hoque, K. (1996). National ownership and HR practices in UK greenfield sites. *Human Resource Management Journal*, 6, 4, 50–74.

Guthrie, J. P., & Olian, J. (1991). Does context affect staffing decisions? The case of general managers. *Personnel Psychology*, 44, 263–292.

Haak-Saheem, W., & Brewster, C. (2017). 'Hidden' expatriates: International mobility in the United Arab Emirates as a challenge to current understanding of expatriation. *Human Resource Management Journal*, 27, 3, 423–439.

Jackson, S. E., & Schuler, R. S. (1995). Understanding human resource management in the context of organizations and their environments. *Annual Review of Psychology*, 46, 237–264.

Mohamed, A. F., Singh, S., Irani, Z., & Darwish, T. K. (2013). An analysis of recruitment, training and retention practices in domestic and multinational enterprises in the country of Brunei Darussalam. *The International Journal of Human Resource Management*, 24, 10, 2054–2081.

Morishima, M. (1995). Embedding HRM in a social context. *British Journal of Industrial Relations*, 33, 4, 617–640.

Singh, S., Wood, G., Darwish, T., Fleming, J., & Mohammed, A. F. (2019). Human resource management in multinational and domestic enterprises: A comparative institutional analysis in Southeast Asia. *Thunderbird International Business Review*, 61, 229–241.

Tayeb, M. H. (1995). The competitive advantage of nations: The role of HRM and its socio-cultural context. *International Journal of Human Resource Management*, 6, 3, 588–605.

Witt, M. A., & Redding, G. (2013). Asian business systems: Institutional comparison, clusters and implications for varieties of capitalism and business systems theory. *Socio-Economic Review*, 11, 2, 265–300.

Witt, M. A., & Redding, G. (2014). Introduction. In M. A. Witt & G. Redding (eds), *The Oxford handbook of Asian business systems*. Oxford: Oxford University Press, pp. 1–8.

2 The Context of Brunei Darussalam

Pengiran Muda Abdul Fattaah and Tamer K Darwish

Introduction

A profile of the country context of Brunei Darussalam is presented in this chapter, including geographic, demographic, historical and legal background. Further, given the fact that oil and gas are both finite resources and in order to counter any negative effects of a potential 'resource curse', we also closely look at the economic system presently prevailing in the country and its efforts in the process of economic diversification as one of Brunei's main objectives, and the contributions of the non-petroleum industries. We also discuss the state of HRM and its development in Brunei, and the rationale for selecting this particular context to conduct our research.

Geographic and Demographic Overview

Brunei Darussalam is a small country located in Southeast Asia. The area comprises a total of 5,765 sq. km of land and a coastline of approximately 161 km running alongside the South China Sea. The South China Sea is located to the north, whilst the Malaysian state of Sarawak is found on all other sides, dividing Brunei Darussalam into two different areas: the Eastern part, which is acknowledged as the Temburong area; and the Western part, comprising the Brunei-Muara, Belait, and Tutong regions.

In terms of population, in 2018 it was estimated that Brunei Darussalam was home to 443,669 inhabitants, comprising 224,053 males and 219,616 females. In terms of race, the most prominent group is Malay, with this particular group including Brunei Malays, Belait, Tutong, Dusuns, Bisayas, Muruts, and Kedayans, as recognised by the Brunei Nationality Act (1961), with the second largest racial group being Chinese. Brunei populations commonly speak Malay, although English is also widely spoken.

A Historical Overview

During the 15th and 16th centuries, the Brunei Empire experienced its Golden Age, a period when its power and influence gradually increased and its territories extended over the whole island of Borneo, including the sultanates of Sambas, Pontianak, Banjarmasin, Pasir Kotai, the Sulu Islands, Palawan, Balabac, and even Manila in the Philippines. During this time, great power was held by Brunei under the fifth sultan, Sultan Bolkiah (1473–1521), who was acknowledged for his seafaring activities and for having captured Manila, even if only fleetingly. Later, the ninth sultan, Sultan Hassan (1605–1619), created a comprehensive Royal Court framework, some of whose distinctive components are still operating today (Hj. Mohd Amin, 1951).

After the demise of Sultan Hassan, Brunei experienced a period of deterioration owing to a number of conflicts and battles over royal succession, compounded by the increasing encroachments of influence by a number of European colonial powers in the arena; these tumultuous events resulted in a number of negative outcomes, including the destruction of Brunei's economic base and the disruption of conventional trading patterns, among other things. Subsequently, in 1839, James Brooke, an English adventurer, assisted the sultan in quelling a rebellion upon his arrival in Borneo. Brooke was later rewarded by being installed as governor and subsequently became 'Rajah' of Sarawak, Northwest Borneo, and the territory under his supervision expanded over a period of time.

At this time, in Northeast Borneo, territorial control was also being expanded by the British North Borneo Company. In 1888, Brunei became a British Protectorate – governed through British control over its external affairs but exercising internal autonomy. Later, in 1906, an additional degree of British control was accepted by Brunei, involving the transfer of executive power to a British Resident, who subsequently provided help and advice on a whole variety of issues except those falling under the category of local customs and religion.

Later in the 20th century, in 1959, Brunei was declared a self-governing state through the promulgation of a new constitution, whilst its defence, foreign affairs, and security remained under the responsibility of Britain. Three years later, in 1962, there was an attempt, eventually abandoned, to introduce a partially elected legislative body, albeit with limited powers. The plan was discarded after the Partai Rakyat Brunei, a dissident political party, initiated a comprehensive, fully equipped uprising, which was subsequently put down with the assistance of UK forces (Bolkiah, 2007) [2]. Furthermore, also during this period, particularly during the late 1950s and early 1960s, all calls for the country to become part of a proposed federation, to be called Malaysia, alongside Sabah and Sarawak, were resisted. The sultan decided that Brunei would continue in its status as an independent state.

In 1967, Sultan Haji Hassanal Bolkiah, the eldest son of Sultan Omar Ali Saifuddien III, became the 29th ruler following his father's abdication. The former sultan held the role of Defence Minister and adopted the royal title of Seri Begawan. A few years later, in 1970, Brunei Town, the country's capital, was renamed Bandar Seri Begawan in honour of the former sultan. The Seri Begawan Sultan [3] passed away 19 years after his abdication in 1986.

One of the most notable events when considering the history of Brunei is the signing of a new treaty of cooperation and friendship between the country and the UK, which occurred on January 4, 1979. Pursuant to that treaty, Brunei regained its independence and Brunei Darussalam was recognised as an independent country as of January 1, 1984.

The Legal System

Brunei Darussalam's legal system is founded on English common law involving a body of written common law judgements and statutes, an independent judiciary, and sultan-enacted legislation. There is also a Supreme Court, through which the judges and Chief Justice are sworn in for a three-year term by the monarch. Importantly, the majority of cases are enforced by the magistrates' court, with more serious cases put before the High Court, which operates for approximately two weeks each month. There is an agreement in place between the UK and Brunei whereby UK judges are appointed to the High Court of Brunei and the Court of Appeal. Moreover, final appeals can also be heard by London's Judicial Committee of the Privy Council, but only in civil, not criminal, matters. Furthermore, Brunei is also known to have a completely distinct system for those cases falling under Sharia law in regard to familial and other Muslim-relevant matters. Markedly, in various arenas, Islamic Sharia law takes precedence over civil laws. Notably, in May, 2014, it was announced in His Majesty's speech that Brunei would implement Sharia law in three phases; as a result, Brunei is becoming the first East Asian country to adopt Sharia law. As of 2019, Sharia law has been fully implemented. This will have a number of implications for the legal system in the country, given that, as stated earlier, in some cases, Islamic Sharia law takes precedence over civil laws in Brunei.

International Affairs and Organisations

Brunei Darussalam is recognised by and is a member of a number of international and regional entities, including APEC, the ADB, ASEAN, the Commonwealth, the ILO, the IMF, the OIC, UNESCAP, UNESCO, the UNSD, and the WTO. In regard to trade, a number of free trade agreements have been reached between Brunei and other countries, including Japan (Brunei-Japan Economic Partnership Agreement); Brunei is also party to the Trans-Pacific Strategic Economic Agreement (which includes the Republic of Chile, New Zealand, and Singapore) and is a member of the ASEAN FTAs, with Australia, China, India, Japan, Korea, and New Zealand.

An Economic Profile

For a number of years, Brunei has been recognised as a valuable player within the ASEAN region, with the country further establishing significant relations with the UK, as can be seen when considering its involvement in Britain's affairs, as well as in those of a number of Asian countries, including Singapore, thus creating a notable increase in commercial activity. Importantly, both oil and liquefied natural gas sectors have dominated the economy since their early discovery in 1963 (Mohamed et al., 2013).

During the mid-2000s, Brunei is known to have experienced growth in terms of its economy, essentially owing to the high gas and oil prices witnessed across the globe. Nevertheless, despite such a surge, recent years show a significant decline. However, it is recognised that although Brunei has one of the lowest GDP growth rates amongst the ASEAN regions, its standing in terms of macroeconomic stability is one of the highest in the world and the highest in Asia. Importantly, Brunei has been protected from a great deal of the impacts of the financial crisis (2008–2009) owing to the government's conservative economic initiatives.

Economic diversification is one of Brunei's main objectives, in consideration of the fact that oil and gas are both finite resources and in order to counter any negative effects of a potential 'resource curse' (Auty, 1993; Darwish et al., 2017); thus, the government has realised that a number of problems might arise should it fail to diversify. Still, during the past ten years, there has been little success noted in this regard, with Brunei's main economic activities remaining centred on the oil and gas sectors.

Taking the above into account, it should be highlighted that there are a number of non-petroleum industries that should receive some degree of attention throughout the process of economic diversification, including agriculture, aquaculture, banking, fishing, and forestry. In terms of textiles, however, since the US removed its garment quota framework at the end of 2004, the garment-for-export industry in Brunei has been experiencing a steady decline. A large number of items need to be imported to Brunei owing to the fact that only a few products, besides petroleum, are produced locally; this is demonstrated by official statistics that show that China, Malaysia, Singapore, and the UK were, in 2018, amongst the leading suppliers of imports. With this in mind, it is pertinent to highlight that the foreign reserves of the country are handled by the Brunei Investment Agency (BIA), which is part of the Ministry of Finance and which adopts the main principle of enhancing the real value of the country's foreign reserves whilst simultaneously following a varied investment approach with holdings in ASEAN countries, Japan, the US, and Western Europe.

Although Brunei has a good basic infrastructure as stated above, high-level infrastructure is still lacking, such as world-class health care, a regional leading university, and a good transportation system (Singh et al., 2019). Brunei is also a very unequal country, ranked 94th in the world; this would suggest that not many people have benefited from the oil and gas boom (Michael, 2018; Singh et al., 2019).

Although its GDP per capita is on a par with that of many developed economies, Brunei is still far from being classified as one of these developed nations. This can largely be explained by looking at the overall developmental indices of the country. Although Brunei's UNDP human development index ranking is reputable, this is mainly because of its high GNP per capita (owing to oil and gas), as the index achieves rather more poorly in relation to other measures such as mean years of schooling (Singh et al., 2017); for instance, a large proportion of the workforce lack basic skills and competencies (UNDP, 2015). Hence, Brunei can be considered both a rich and a poor country, where, outside the oil and gas industries, the country is closer to many developing nations than the developed world (Bryane, 2014). As a matter of fact, the indices of political voice and accountability, and the inegalitarian distribution of political rights, place it at a substantial distance from the developed nations (Chongvilavan, 2014; Singh et al., 2017).

Industry Importance

Oil and Gas

Much like a number of other oil-producing countries, Brunei's economy has experienced both the ups and the downs of the global oil market, with a 2.8% average increase in economic growth experienced in the 2000s, and is marked by a remarkable reliance on the production of oil and gas (Darwish et al., 2017). Brunei is recognised as the third-largest producer of oil in the Southeast Asian region, with the number of barrels produced each day in 2018 amounting to approximately 180,000. The main export destinations include ASEAN countries, South Korea, Japan, Taiwan, and the US. Moreover, in terms of liquefied natural gas exportation, Brunei is known to be the ninth largest exporter, with the majority being exported to Japan and South Korea. Generally, it is known that, during recent years, there has been a decrease in oil and gas production. With this in mind, it is pertinent to highlight that, whilst natural gas reserves are expected to last 40 years, oil is expected to last only another quarter of a century. It is expected that reserve sources will increase with the implementation of new technology alongside potential deep sea and onshore fields.

Notably, this over-reliance on the oil and gas industries has affected the development of the private sector in Brunei. In fact, the non-oil and -gas sectors have steadily contributed around 20% to GDP in recent years (OECD, 2014; Darwish et al., 2017). As a result, the country now has a larger government sector, which has limited the role of the private sector and the opportunities it can offer (Darwish et al., 2017). The oil and gas industries' dominance is further strengthened by high wages for labour and low productivity, an issue that makes the majority of the private sector internationally uncompetitive (Lawrey, 2010; OECD, 2014).

Brunei's main oil and gas production company is a joint venture owned equally by the Royal Dutch/Shell group of companies and the Brunei government, and is known as Brunei Shell Petroleum (BSP). The organisation also operates the country's only refinery. This company is very important in terms of Brunei's economy owing to the fact that alongside its four sister organisations – including BLNG, a company producing liquefied natural gas – BSP is the second largest employer in the country, second only to the government. Importantly, although the refinery only has the capacity to distil 10,000 barrels each day, this is nevertheless recognised as adequate to fulfil petroleum product demand in the domestic context.

Importantly, most of Brunei's natural gas is liquefied at BLNG, which was first established in 1972 and is nowadays one of the major global LNG plants, with approximately 90% of the country's LNG subsequently being sold to Japan as a result of a long-standing agreement between the two countries that was further renewed in 1992. Notably, this particular arrangement requires Brunei to deliver in excess of 6 million tons of LNG to three key Japanese utilities – namely, the Tokyo Electric Power Company (TEPCO), the Tokyo Gas Company, and the Osaka Gas Company – on an annual basis. Moreover, also in regard to Brunei LNG, Brunei Coldgas, and Brunei Shell Tankers, there is a joint venture in place between Shell, the Brunei government, and the Japanese organisation Mitsubishi to produce LNG and ensure its delivery to Japan. Furthermore, since 1995, the Korea Gas Corporation has also been supplied with 700,000 tons of LNG from Brunei each year. Notably, only a small proportion of natural gas is utilised for domestic power generation. With such figures in mind, it is important to recognise Japan's standing in terms of natural gas, as it is known to be the main export market.

Non-oil and –Gas Sector Industries

Since the beginning of the 21st century, Brunei's government has made several attempts to ensure economic diversification. Undoubtedly, the country is in a good position to achieve such a goal owing to oil and gas sales and associated revenue and numerous investments made outside of the country. Notably, the financial sector, the industrial sector (beyond gas and oil), and the tourism and hospitality sectors have all received attention from the Brunei government.

The Financial Sector

Since 2002, there have been numerous changes across the financial sector, particularly following the government's attempts to develop Brunei not only as a centre for Islamic banking but also as a global offshore financial centre. Efforts began in 2000, at which time the country's government introduced a tax-advantaged International Financial Centre (IFC). Beforehand, the area was already recognised as an active commercial centre, and it is now serviced by a large number of banking institutions, as can be seen when considering the present active involvement of a number of entities – namely HSBC, Standard Chartered, Citibank, Overseas Union Bank, RHB, and Maybank – within the sector. Presently, only two local banks are operating, namely the Islamic Bank of Brunei Darussalam and Baiduri Bank, the former being an Islamic bank and the latter a private bank. Given the regulations and statutes implemented in a number of Middle Eastern petro-states, such local banking entities are likely to be preferred by foreign investors with large-scale projects.

There has been a surge in the Islamic banking sector within Brunei and surrounding areas, with business incorporation and offshore banking remaining a relatively small sector in the general financial services sector. With this in mind, conservatively but assertively, Brunei declared its aim to utilise its human resources, sovereignty, and wealth; thus, Brunei IFC has now implemented a number of international regulations devised with careful consideration to facilitate cost-effective, flexible capabilities that are modern and innovative. In this context, it was communicated that Brunei would adopt a dual jurisdiction, with international legislation delivering not only the usual range of domestic legislations, such as those adopted in England and Wales, but also international legislation aimed at delivering offshore facilities.

On January 1, 2011, the government founded the Brunei Monetary Authority (AMBD), which constitutes Brunei Darussalam's central bank and is primarily concerned with the establishment and application of monetary policies, the regulation and supervision of financial entities, and the management of currency.

Tourism and Hospitality Sector

Brunei's government has similarly acknowledged the significant potential associated with tourism, as has been noted by Tan and Omar Ali (1998); thus, the improvement of more traditional locations, including museums, mosques, and water villages, for example, as well as the promotion of localised activities, such as river cruises and game fishing, has also resulted in a number of ecotourism programmes being implemented with the aim of making the most of the country's untouched tropical rainforest, which occupies more than 70% of the country's land.

Markedly, a number of efforts and attempts have been made to take advantage of the location of the country and to provide tourists with access to a number of other destinations, thus enhancing the hotel industry and further encouraging modernisation. Importantly, such initiatives complement the goal of Brunei to act as a key service hub for both tourism and trade, in addition to being recognised as a communications, trade, and logistics centre.

Industrial Sector

As the government strives to implement economic diversification within Brunei, industry has gained momentum as the most realistic and viable way of achieving this aim. Accordingly, numerous efforts have been made by the government to emphasise the industrial niche, including capital-intensive industries, environmentally acceptable industries, and high-value-added industries, as well as export-orientated economic activities. Moreover, although it is acknowledged that Brunei is geared towards achieving development of small- to medium-sized enterprises (SMEs), and has accordingly developed a technology incubator with the aim of promoting the IT industry and its development, it is nevertheless recognised that the country requires significant government involvement in order to achieve this aim. With this in mind, over the last ten years there has been much investment by the government in a world-class methanol plant, which has been established through a joint venture with a number of Japanese organisations and the Brunei Methanol Company, necessitating the investment of more than half a billion US dollars. Furthermore, the government has announced a project of up to BND 6 billion that will involve the development of a chemical plant and numerous refineries at the new Pulau Muara Besar (PMB) industrial site, to be implemented by a Chinese organisation. It is the hope of the Brunei government that such initiatives will induce downstream industries, which could potentially achieve economic diversification.

The Importance of HRM in the Context of Brunei

Economic diversification and maturity are two key objectives of the country and are believed to be realistic goals in view of the GDP per capita, which is recognised as exceeding that of most developing world countries, in addition to the notable income garnered through overseas investments, which is added to domestic production revenues. However, several leaders within the country hold that continuously increasing integration into the world economy could potentially weaken internal social consistency; this has resulted in the creation of a model aimed at assisting the country's long-term development.

Brunei Darussalam's Long-Term Development Framework

In 2007, a 30-year development framework was established, comprising 'Wawasan Brunei 2035', the Outline of Strategies and Policies for Development (OSPD), and the National Development Plan (NDP/RKN). The first of these is considered to be a national vision concerned with facilitating the nation to achieve a reputation for educated and highly skilled professionals according to internationally recognised standards, delivering quality of life, and ensuring a sustainable and dynamic economy with good levels of income per capita.

In order for the three aforementioned outcomes to be achieved, a number of approaches have been devised so as to facilitate the systematic and effective implementation of all development-related elements. These approaches include strategies for the economy, education, the environment, infrastructure development, institutional development, local business development, security, and social security.

The RKN is revised every five years, with the fifth restatement, RKN5 (2007–2012) being the first to be devised in regard to the 'Wawasan Brunei 2035' objectives. The previous four were essentially concerned with enhancing people's quality of life, developing non-oil industries, maintaining full employment, maintaining a moderate rate of inflation, encouraging and nurturing the development of 'Rakyat Melayu' as commerce and industry leaders, maximising the economic utilisation of natural resources, accelerating human resource development (HRD), increasing productivity, fostering a more caring, disciplined and self-reliant society, and ensuring a clean and healthy environment.

Following two decades of development in terms of the previous four RKNs, spanning the period 1986–2005, there were only modest attainments in terms of the economic utilisation of resources, HRD, increased levels of productivity, and maintenance of full employment. Undoubtedly, there were a number of notable outcomes in terms of enhancing quality of life, ensuring a clean and healthy environment, and maintaining low inflation rates. Although progress in regard to non-oil industry development; the development of the 'Rakyat Melayu' as industry and commerce leaders; and the establishment of a caring, disciplined, and self-reliant society was relatively slow.

Furthermore, in regard to the economy, development has been unpredictable and has varied, with weakness and vulnerabilities witnessed in Brunei's economy following the growth of the early 1990s. With this in mind, at the end of the RKN8 period, during 2005, Brunei Darussalam's nominal GDP was BND 15.9 billion. At around the same time, GDP per capita was approximately BND 43,000, which was 35% higher than the figure for 2000, which was BND 32,000. Furthermore, the contribution to GDP made by the gas and oil sectors was approximately 54.1%, despite it being 57.5% in 2000 at the end of RKN7. In real terms, GDP growth averaged just 2.1% each year during the period of the RKN8, which is recognised as being lower than the targeted annual growth rate by around 5%–6%. As a result, Brunei Darussalam witnessed slower economic growth compared with worldwide growth, which was approximately 3.8% annually during 2000–2005, and it was even slower compared with the approximate 5% growth achieved by ASEAN during the same period.

In consideration of the notable reliance on fiscal stimulus by Brunei Darussalam's economy, lower economic growth has been witnessed following various development project delays, which undoubtedly restricts the overall efficiency of the government's adopted fiscal stimulus approach. In this regard, one of the main issues concerned with enhancing the growth rates of the economy during RKNS 2007–2012 was the enhancement of national capacity to ensure that development initiatives can be implemented. In this regard, one of the key development objectives during the next five-year period is concerned with strengthening institutions. Furthermore, bureaucratic processes, which are able to establish the effectiveness of government operations, will be simplified in order to enhance the overall efficiency and quality of project implementation.

In regard to the above aim, a number of needs should be taken into account when formulating the development agenda, namely the need to ensure implementation enhancements, consideration of any barriers or obstructions to achieving high economic growth and socio-economic development, and the need to fulfil the goals of 'Wawasan Brunei 2035'.

Essentially, development is multifaceted and thus necessitates the careful organisation of government policies and initiatives. Importantly, government policies and programmes and their cross-cutting nature must reflect the policy directions detailed within the OSPD; therefore, all projects and programmes should be designed in consideration of four key objectives:

1   To widen the economic base and thereby reinforce and support the underpinning of a knowledge-based economy (KBE). This is essential when considering the nation's small natural resources benefaction, as well as its population and geographic size. Creativity, innovation, and knowledge are fundamental aspects of a KBE, and so it will be adopted as a driver for enhancing economic diversification.
2   To maintain political stability and enhance social progress.
3   To increase the number of highly skilled and educated professionals in the labour force, considering the main aim of the 2007–2012 RKNS, which centres on HRD.
4   To strengthen institutional capacity in view of the acknowledgement that seamless bureaucratic and competent civil service processes are fundamental to the effective application of the RKNS 2007–2012 initiative.

The Privatisation Master Plan will be adopted by the government and will include the vision, policy, strategy, and long-term privatisation programme for Brunei, with further consideration to the coordination, implementation, planning, and monitoring of the programme. Moreover, the government is also concerned with enhancing its attempts to attract foreign direct investment (FDI), which will be achieved through various measures – including competitive incentive packages; skilled and productive human resources; investment policies and regulations; more globalised SMEs; and provision of world-class infrastructure, sufficient legal infrastructure, and transparent procedures.

Rationale of the Context

Through the numerous research studies carried out on HRM, it has been established that a great deal of emphasis is placed on the national context in addition to conditional variables that establish HRM policies and practices, as highlighted by Boxall (1995), Brewster et al. (1996), and Budhwar and Debrah (2001). With this in mind, a number of national elements, including culture, economic landscape, and institutional arrangements, may all have some degree of impact on the HRM practices and policies adopted by businesses (Brewster, 1995; Sparrow, 1995; Tayeb, 1995). Accordingly, there is a need to carry out further studies in a number of different contexts, as has been highlighted by various scholars in the field (Meyer, 2006; Darwish et al., 2017). Therefore, the present book focuses on Brunei Darussalam, which is recognised as being far removed from a Western context and is thus an entirely new and interesting area of investigation.

In addition, Brunei is currently at the beginning of its efforts to achieve development, which is recognised as an entirely novel circumstance in the context of this country since it gained independence in 1984. In this same vein, in 2009 the IMF established a report that highlighted the long-term obstacles and barriers the country would face, including the need to enhance fiscal management, diversify the economy, and expand gas and oil reserves. Essentially, these problems are the same for all countries with a great dependence on certain finite resources. However, following a number of years of failure in regard to diversification, the government of Brunei has recently implemented a series of efforts to harmonise and coordinate oil and gas sector activities with those of the private sector, with the aim of enhancing downstream industries' activities.

Another reason for carrying out the current work is Brunei's geographic proximity to other Asian countries. As has been highlighted, Brunei is part of ASEAN and is active in terms of trading. Importantly, despite the fact that ASEAN has been operating for a number of years, the rules and regulations associated with the trading block are still undergoing development, as are organisational partner relationships, including those with China, Europe, and the US. In this respect, studies have been carried out in relation to a number of other ASEAN countries, although Brunei is unique in this regard. For example, Tasie (2009) carried out a study on diversification in Brunei and found that the country is notably protected from globalisation impacts and is therefore not seen to have shared in the development and growth of neighbouring countries, including Indonesia, Malaysia, Singapore, and Thailand.

Furthermore, the majority of studies carried out in relation to HRM in non-industrialised countries have mainly focused on the industrial sector; in contrast, we consider all industries within the country where HRM is a consideration. It is believed that this will help to garner a more wide-ranging perspective and degree of understanding. Undoubtedly, the country is recognised as an area undergoing rapid economic diversification; thus, owing to Brunei's strategic location and the fact that it is a key member of the ASEAN trading block, it is believed that this book will provide notable contributions to HRM, particularly in the context of Asia.

Summary

This chapter has delivered an overview and some degree of insight in relation to Brunei. This has been achieved by providing a geographic and demographic overview, a historical background, and an outline of the current legal system. This gives an insight into the systems inherent in the country, which closely follow governing systems found in the UK.

We have also strongly emphasised the economic environment, looking closely at the oil and gas sector, as well as the other industries found in the country. We have shown the country's reliance on the oil and gas sector and the benefits that high oil prices have brought for the GDP and international standing of the country. We have also shown how this reliance has inadvertently caused other sectors to stagnate, with any activities in these sectors needing government projects and public funding to grow. Furthermore, there has been consideration of the needs and plans of the country, with human resource and industrial development plans explained and described. This emphasises the need to develop the country's human resources to cope with the planned economic diversification away from its reliance on the oil and gas sector.

This chapter also highlights justifications and the rationale for selecting Brunei as a case study. The country is still developing and has characteristics that have not been explored deeply in the field of HRM. Its close vicinity to the ASEAN economies, which have shown high levels of growth, and the level of diversification already in progress, make the context of interest to researchers in the field of HRM.

References

Auty, R. (1993). *Sustaining development in mineral economies: The resource curse thesis*. London: Routledge.

Bolkiah, M. (2007). *Remember, remember, the 8th of December*. Brunei Darussalam: Brunei Press.

Boxall, P. (1995). Building the theory of comparative HRM. *Human Resource Management Journal*, 6, 3, 59–75.

Brewster, C. (1995). HRM: The European dimension. In J. Storey (ed.), *Human resource management: A critical text*, 309–331. London: Routledge.

Brewster, C., Tregaskis, O., Hegewisch, A., & Mayne, L. (1996). Comparative research in human resource management: A review and an example. *International Journal of Human Resource Management*, 7, 3, 585–604.

Bryane, M. (2014). What does Brunei teach us about using human development index rankings as a policy tool? University of Hong Kong. http://papers.ssrn.com/sol3/papers.cfm?abstract_id=2395661

Budhwar, P., & Debrah, Y. (2001). Rethinking comparative and cross national human resource management research. *International Journal of Human Resource Management*, 12, 3, 497–515.

Chongvilavan, A. (2014). Inequality in South East Asia. In R. Kanbur, R. Rhee, & J. Zhuang (eds), *Inequality in the Asia Pacific*. Abingdon: Routledge, pp. 303–328.

Darwish, T., Mohamed, A. F., Wood, G., Singh, S., & Fleming, J. (2017). Can HRM alleviate the negative effects of the resource curse on firms? Evidence from Brunei. *Personnel Review*, 46, 8, 1931–1947.

Hj. Mohd Amin, M. R. (1951). *Stories of Brunei Darussalam – its laws and customs*. Brunei Darussalam: State Secretary's Office.

Lawrey, R. N. (2010). An economist's perspective on economic diversification in Brunei Darussalam. *CSPS Strategy and Policy Journal*, 1, 13–28.

Meyer, K. E. (2006). Asian management research needs more self-confidence. *Asia Pacific Journal of Management*, 23, 119–127.

Michael, B. (2018). What does Brunei teach us about using Human Development Index rankings as a policy tool? *Development Policy Review*, 36, O414–O431.

Mohamed, A. F., Singh, S., Irani, Z., & Darwish, T. (2013). An analysis of recruitment, training and retention practices in domestic and multinational enterprises in the country of Brunei Darussalam. *The International Journal of Human Resource Management*, 24, 10, 2054–2081.

Singh, S., Darwish, T., Wood, G., & Mohamed, A. F. (2017). Institutions, complementarity, human resource management and performance in a South-East Asian petrostate: The case of Brunei. *The International Journal of Human Resource Management*, 28, 18, 2538–2569.

Singh, S., Wood, G., Darwish, T., Fleming, J., & Mohammed, A. F. (2019). Human resource management in multinational and domestic enterprises: A comparative institutional analysis in Southeast Asia. *Thunderbird International Business Review*, 61, 229–241.

Sparrow, P. R. (1995). Towards a dynamic and comparative model of European human resource management: An extended review. *International Journal of Human Resource Management*, 6, 481–505.

Tan, S. E., & Omar Ali, H. N. (1998). The hotel industry in Negara Brunei Darussalam. *Borneo Review*, 9, 2, 99–122.

Tasie, G. (2009). Can Japanese management styles be applied to Africa? *African Journal of Business Management*, 3, 4, 233–239.

Tayeb, M. H. (1995). The competitive advantage of nations: The role of HRM and its socio-cultural context. *International Journal of Human Resource Management*, 6, 3, 588–605.

The economic outlook for Southeast Asia, China and India (2014). *Beyond the middle-income trap.* doi:10.1787/saeo-2014-en

UNDP (2015). *Human development reports.* http://hdr.undp.org/en/content/table-1-human-development-index-and-its-components

3 Comparative Human Resource Management

Chris Brewster and Washika Haak-Saheem

Introduction

This chapter explores the differences between the way that countries manage their human resources. Despite the growing process of globalisation, the chapter argues that context still matters. Further, we explain how different countries have different notions of 'human resource management (HRM)' and what it means, how it is understood, and what would be considered effective HRM policies and practices. These differences present a challenge to multinational enterprises (MNEs) managing workers in different countries (see chapter on international human resource management (IHRM)). And significantly, comparative HRM is a challenge to the universalist paradigm of HRM, generally expressed in the notion of best practice. Given the comparative lens, comparative HRM argues that the subject has to be seen within its contextual setting, including both the internal context, such as leadership style, level, or organisation, and the external environment, such as the national culture or national institutional factors.

Context is a critical factor influencing management in general (Bamberger, 2008) and HRM in particular (Cooke, 2018). It is argued that the outcomes of HRM should be measured via its long-term effects on organisational effectiveness, and individual and societal well-being (Beer, Boselie, & Brewster, 2015). These long-term effects have been ignored in the universalist approach to strategic human resource management (SHRM). Scholars and practitioners must develop a solid understanding of the specifications of the contextual environment in order to foster HRM practices that are sustainable and of benefit for all stakeholders. In addition to the strong interest of comparative HRM in how HRM in different countries emerges over time, it is of relevance to examine whether existing HRM practices evolve towards a common model.

The globalisation, or convergence, debate is a fundamental topic in comparative HRM. Beyond cross-sectional research methodologies providing statistical snapshots of commonalities and differences, addressing this issue requires longitudinal analyses. Such analyses have been greatly helped through the data collection efforts of Cranet (www.cranet.org), which has provided the comparative HRM field with 40 years of widely representative country-comparative HRM data at five-year time intervals. This has encouraged studies in comparative HRM to address core questions about developments in HRM over time, thus providing insights into the convergence-divergence debate. The convergence argument is driven largely by the economic and general management literature (Uzzi, 1996; Drezner, 2001; Mayrhofer et al., 2011), which argues that the forces of globalisation will create management practices that become increasingly similar as a result of increased use around the world of very similar technologies and communication. This is reflected in the comparative HRM literature, where 'dominance effects' have been identified (Smith & Meiksins, 1995; Pudelko & Harzing, 2007), whereby those models that have been viewed as most successful have exemplary power in other communities, setting standards for the other countries. Another strand argues that regions are more important. The influence of the European Union on HRM has been profound, enforcing common legislation on contractual terms, on discrimination, on health and safety, and on communication requirements, for example. Rather than global convergence, this strand of comparative HRM research suggests that over time we will witness regional convergence, with the regions becoming increasingly differentiated. However, other discussion within comparative HRM argues that we should not expect any convergence at all (Dunphy, 1987; Paik, Vance, & Stage, 1996; Brewster, Mayrhofer, & Farndale, 2018).

Generally speaking, both the cultural literature (López-Duarte, Vidal-Suárez, & González-Díaz, 2016; Cooke, Veen, & Wood, 2017) and the institutional literature (Meyer, 2015; Adams, Smart, & Huff, 2017) argue that countries are distinctive and change only slowly, and that any change over time is path-dependent.

Contextualising HRM leads to at least three questions. First, can HRM in different contexts be conducted in a similar way or does it have to adapt to the respective circumstances? Behind this question lurks the discussion about best practice vs best fit, i.e., is there one best model of HRM, as is often assumed in US-based HR concepts, or is it necessary to take into account contextual specifics in order to achieve the best outcome? Second, what are the crucial forces leading to HRM-relevant contextual differences? The two major factors are culture and institutions. Third, how do similarities and differences between various contexts develop over time? Taking a temporal perspective, the issues of convergence, divergence, or stasis arise, i.e., will the different contexts – most often countries – become more alike or more different, or stay relatively stable.

This chapter addresses these questions, first by exploring some of the key scholarly discussions in comparative HRM. These are the conceptual paradigms that underlie how the topic is understood, the issue of convergence and divergence, and the issue of the explanatory factors for the differences that are found. These conceptual differences provide a platform on which to explore some of the differences in the way that human resources are managed in different countries.

The Concepts Behind Comparative HRM

'When in Rome, do as the Romans do'. This applies to the ways HRM is conceptualised, the research traditions through which it is explored, and the way HRM is performed. In conceptual and research terms, two different (ideal type) paradigms have been identified as the universalist and the contextual (Brewster, 1999). Early research referred to the notion of paradigms in the context of HRM (Delery & Doty, 1996). In this chapter, the universalist and contextual paradigms will serve as good examples, building as they do on the significant US and northern European traditions.

The universalist paradigm, which tends to dominate in the US is also widely used in other countries, is essentially a nomothetic social science approach: it uses (empirical) evidence to test generalisations of an abstract and law-like character. With reference to other areas in the social sciences, the universalist paradigm tends to result in convergence. This paradigm assumes that the purpose of the study of our area of the social sciences, HRM, and, in particular, SHRM (Younger, Smallwood, & Ulrich, 2007; Delery & Roumpi, 2017) is to improve the way that human resources are managed strategically within organisations, with little reference to contextual factors. In this view, the ultimate aim is to improve organisational performance (Huselid, 1995) or the customer experience (Ulrich, Brockbank & Yeung, 1989), or to serve shareholders' interests (Becker & Gerhart, 1996; Guest, 1997). Further, this debate assumes that this objective will apply in all cultural and institutional contexts. The value of this paradigm is its simplicity, the merging of research around this shared view, and the clear relationship with the interest of practitioner-managers. The disadvantages lie in the ignoring of other potential focuses, the limitation on research objectives, and the ignoring of other levels of analysis and other stakeholders, such as communities (Beer, Boselie, & Brewster, 2015; Guest, 2017). Arguably, there is greater coherence in the US over what constitutes best practice in HRM: an evolving view around the notion of high-performance work systems (Becker & Huselid, 2006). Pfeffer (1998) suggests the following seven principles as conditions of successful organisations:

- Employment security
- Selective hiring of new personnel
- Self-managed teams and decentralisation of decision-making as the basic principles of organisational design

- Comparatively high compensation contingent on organisational performance
- Extensive training
- Reduced status distinctions and barriers, including dress, language, office arrangements, and wage differences across levels
- Extensive sharing of financial and performance information throughout the organisation.

Similar to other studies in the field of SHRM, Pfeffer (1998) argues that organisational success is determined by the right set of HRM principles. Perhaps in a country like the US, where there is widespread agreement that external factors, such as government regulation, trade unions, etc., should not be allowed to impact on business, there is some sense in developing a vision of HRM that takes as its scope simply the policies and practices of management.

By contrast, the contextual paradigm is idiographic; it seeks an overall understanding of what is contextually unique and why. In the field of comparative HRM, it aims to develop a better understanding of what varies between and within HRM in various contexts and what drives the differences (Paauwe & Farndale, 2017). Often, the research methods used are inductive. Most of the literature highlighting the need for a more contextual paradigm research considers the link between HRM and firm performance to be secondary (see, e.g., Beer, Boselie, & Brewster, 2015). It is assumed that HRM can apply to societies, governments, or regions as well as to firms. At the level of the organisation, the firm's objectives and strategy are not necessarily assumed to be good or bad for the organisation or for society: they have to be assessed in terms of their outcomes. Nor, in this paradigm, is there any assumption that the interests of everyone in the organisation will be the same, nor any expectation that an organisation will have a strategy that people within the organisation will support (see, e.g., Guest, 2017).

The contextual paradigm emphasises external factors as well as the management policies and practices within an organisation. Thus, it considers the importance of such factors as national culture, ownership structures, labour market structure, and the role of the state and trade unions. The scope of HRM, it is argued, should reflect the reality of the role of many HRM specialists. For example, Haak-Saheem and Festing (2016) show empirically how institutional factors such as the role of the state shape HRM. This paradigm is widespread in European countries, and more widely, for example, in Australia and New Zealand.

In summary, cultural and institutional views are fundamental to the comparative HRM approach. Comparative HRM uses these theories to understand differences between nations. Both approaches are relevant to understanding what is happening in HRM.

Cultural and Institutional Factors Shaping HRM

Because we know that there are differences in the way that countries understand and practise HRM, what are the reasons for these differences? Generally, speaking, there are two competing sets of explanators: the cultural and the institutional. If the differences in the meaning, objectives, practices, and outcomes of HRM between nations are accepted, then the next step is to develop a better understanding of the reasons for, or the antecedents of, these differences. The cultural and institutional frameworks are broad categorisations and within each field there is a raft of competing and often incompatible theories. It is argued that different values and different relationships between people are clustered in countries and, inevitably, reflected in the way that people manage other people.

Fukuyama (1995) argues that organisations represent cultural communities of rational utility-maximising individuals. Practices will vary with cultural context. Typically, these variations will reflect national boundaries, but this is by no means always the case. Thus, countries like Belgium or Spain contain communities speaking different languages, with different religions and different legislation, seeming, at least to the citizens there, sharply different in their approaches to life. Cultural groups in the Middle East and Africa were divided by the colonial map-makers and may have more in common with groups in countries across national borders than they do with other citizens of their own country (Wood et al., 2011; Haak-Saheem & Festing, 2016).

Whilst the cultural approach is an extremely broad one, it may be possible for a society to enhance its social capital, though it is not possible to develop social trust deliberately and systematically, or radically depart from established rules and norms (Fukuyama, 1995). Culture is viewed as being shared by individuals as a means of conferring meaning on, and adding sense to, social interactions. Even if the nature of that culture may be relatively fluid and subjective, it provides a persistent boundary to the life of individuals and clusters thereof.

Previous research found geographically based, usually national, differences in what is appropriate and not appropriate in particular contexts (Hofstede, 2001). These perceptions affect the way people in a country see and interpret the world. Schwartz (1999) and Sagiv and Schwartz (2007) emphasise the interrelation between cultural-level and individual-level values: each individual will be different but the aggregation of their approaches makes what is acceptable and desirable in one country different from what is acceptable or desirable in another. Because HRM is concerned with interactions between people at different hierarchical levels within an organisation, these cultural differences will inevitably be reflected in differences in the way people are managed.

In contrast to the cultural view, the institutional perspective argues that institutions within a society are the main factor influencing HRM

(Vaiman & Brewster, 2015). Social arrangements in a nation are always distinct and many of the institutions are likely to shape the social construction of an organisation. For example, the general and vocational education system, the way labour markets work and employment legislation will all impact on the way that HRM practices are applied (Björkman, Fey, & Park, 2007). Thus, HRM has be considered as a function of the country's particular institutional arrangements (Haak-Saheem & Festing, 2016). As with the cultural effects, there seems to be a kind of societal recipe that it is possible to go against, or ignore, but only at a cost. Most people, or most organisations, do not do so.

The institutional view within the management literature is not new (Rosenzweig & Singh, 1991). In particular, patterns of ownership vary (Brewster, 2007). Whilst public ownership has decreased to some extent in many European countries in recent years, large corporations in emerging economies – in the Gulf States, for example – are owned by the government (Haak-Saheem, Festing & Darwish, 2017).

Whilst each stream of thought generally gives no more than a passing nod to the other view, it seems that neither an exclusively culturalist nor an exclusively institutional approach is helpful in the context of comparative HRM. Many of the cultural writers see institutions as key artefacts of culture that reflect deep underlying variations in the values across societies; many institutional writers include culture as one of the institutional elements explaining differences.

Both institutional and cultural accounts assume strong path dependence: neither institutions nor culture can be readily changed. This may easily lead to assumptions that countries characterised by poor economic performance are in some manner defective, and that others may be so irrevocably different as to preclude sustainable and peaceful long-term economic relations (McSweeney, 2012). Again, the fact that many national boundaries do not always coincide with ethnic variations has not prevented scholars from categorising cultural characteristics according to country (McSweeney, 2012).

However, even given these limitations, the institutional approach offers a wider range of explanations. For example, Wood et al. (2012) note that the new institutionalism is at least as multifaceted as the cultural literature and has similar problems of definition and measurement. However, they also note that there is a consistency to the notion that certain factors within society create a degree of isomorphism in organisations searching for legitimacy and resources (DiMaggio & Powell, 1983) and that this in turn creates a certain path dependence in the directions that the society can take. As Hollingsworth (2006) suggests, it is likely that national institutional frameworks evolve in a nonlinear fashion that combines continuity with change. Vaiman and Brewster (2015) argue that companies have considerable, if not unlimited, scope to manage cultural differences, but fewer opportunities to ignore educational systems, labour markets, government regulations, legislation, and other institutional aspects of a society.

Overall, the interests of shareholders play a prominent role in this literature (Jackson & Deeg, 2008) and they have also been given prominence in the comparative capitalisms literature, although the latter sees societal restraints on shareholder rights as being potentially beneficial, rather than pathological. Hence, comparative capitalisms theory makes a distinction between the liberal market economies (LMEs) of the Anglo-Saxon world and the coordinated market economies (CMEs) of the Rhineland, Scandinavia, and Japan (Hall & Soskice, 2001). For LMEs, shareholder value is pre-eminent, contractual relationships tend to be short-term and are trumped by the need for competition, and the government is expected to play only a facilitating role (Wilkinson & Wood, 2017). In CMEs, relationships between organisations are less competitive and adversarial, and the government accepts more responsibility for the way business is conducted (which is meant to be in the interests of a wider group of stakeholders than just the owners of the business) and for the way people at work are treated (Hall & Soskice, 2001; Wood & Lane, 2012). According to Hall and Soskice (2001), the complementarity of institutional factors at either end of the scale allows for successful economies, but between the two extremes, societies will find it difficult to be economically successful and will be pressured to move in one direction or the other.

These dichotomous models have been found wanting by other authors (Whitley, 1999; Amable, 2003), who have argued that the mature economies cannot be readily divided into two archetypes, and that countries that fall in neither category will not necessarily converge towards one or the other. Amable (2003) divides the CME category up between the developed East Asian economies, Scandinavia, the Mediterranean economies, and the Rhineland economies.

The models that we have so far tend to be very Eurocentric, meaning that they ignore most of the world (Jackson & Deeg, 2008). Recently there have been attempts to explore national business systems in the Arab Gulf States (Haak-Saheem & Festing, 2016) or Africa, labelled as segmented business systems (Wood & Frynas, 2006).

Despite the wealth of literature on institutionalism, it has remained difficult to explain internal diversity of market economies (Walker, Brewster, & Wood, 2014). The early literature on comparative capitalism tended to take a static view, because societies were conceived of as consisting of reinforcing complementarities, which makes it difficult to explain systemic change (Streeck & Thelen, 2005). Some of the criticisms of these comparative capitalisms theories have also come from people concerned about the mismatch between the theoretical attempt to explain firm-level behaviour and the fact that much of the evidence adduced is drawn from broad trends in labour markets, legalisation, limited panels of case studies and/or broad macroeconomic indicators (Wood et al., 2011). In other words, although the literature on comparative capitalism makes broad assumptions as to how work and employment relations vary from setting to setting, there is very little on what really goes on inside the firm (Wood et al., 2011).

Convergence and Divergence in HRM

The convergence-divergence debate has been an ongoing issue in international management (Fenton-O'Creevy & Gooderham, 2003) and presents the argument that the patterns of organisational and institutional behaviours within industrial societies have been 'converging' or becoming more similar. When researchers began first to study the management of organisations in different countries, the belief was that management principles would hold universally (Gooderham & Brewster, 2003). The convergence-divergence debate highlights the arguments that HRM within organisations will become increasingly similar due to firms having structures that are free from cultural influences and are more affected by more tangible influences such as industry, size, and technology, with globalisation freeing MNEs from the influence of national institutions; this has renewed interest in the convergence hypothesis (Farndale et al., 2017).

Early management researchers assumed that organisational practices would converge towards the most efficient model, which would therefore, they argued, be the US model (Smith & Meiksins, 1995; Pudelko, 2005). More recently, the convergence thesis has received support from transaction cost economics, which argues that there always exists a best solution to organising labour (Williamson, 1985). Benchmarking practices in organisations focus on the diffusion of best practice (Wright & Brewster, 2003). They have doubtless contributed to shaping similar forms of organisation across countries as well as similar curricula in business education.

Most of these views nowadays centre on convergence towards a US model – the model of the most powerful country in the world (Smith & Meiksins, 1995). Previously, the dominant model was that of Japan and it may, in the not-too-distant future, be that of China. However, at present, one theoretical possibility is that as policies of market deregulation and state decontrol are spreading from the US to Europe and elsewhere, firms everywhere will move towards North American HRM.

Another possibility is that different regional models of HRM may be created. The increasing economic and political integration of the European Union (EU) countries, for example, may cause a convergence, within Europe, towards a distinct European model of HRM. In Europe, 27 countries, currently, are engaged in a historically unique collaboration: they have agreed to subordinate national legislative decision-making to European-level legislation. These developments have indirect effects upon the way people are managed as a result of political and economic integration and direct effects through the EU's adoption of a distinct social sphere of activity. The advent of the EU, providing institutional arrangements at the supra-national level, may, through such developments, support an institutional branch of convergence theory (Gooderham & Brewster, 2003).

There is also a third theoretical possibility: that organisations are so locked into their respective national institutional settings that no common model is likely to emerge for the foreseeable future. Because HRM systems reflect national institutional contexts and cultures, which do not respond readily to the imperatives of technology or the market, each country will continue to be distinctive (DiMaggio & Powell, 1983). The literature often refers to divergence theories, but what is usually meant is 'non-convergence': no one is arguing that countries are becoming even more dissimilar – just that they remain distinctive in the way that they manage their HRM. Managers in each country operate within a specific national institutional context and have a shared set of cultural assumptions. Neither institutions nor cultures change quickly, and they rarely do so in ways that are the same as in other countries. It follows that managers and workers within any one country behave differently from managers in other countries. More importantly, change is path-dependent. In other words, even when change does occur it can be understood only in relation to the specific social context in which it occurs. Even superficially universal principles (profit or efficiency) may be interpreted differently in different countries (Hofstede, 2001).

Attempts have been made to develop a more nuanced theory of convergence (Brewster, Mayrhofer, & Morley, 2004; Farndale et al., 2017). These authors develop a distinction between directional convergence (whether countries share the same trend) and final convergence (whether they are becoming more alike) and also analyse the extent of convergence, arguing that you can have more or less rather than just all or none. In the literature, evidence of similarity in HRM between countries, or similar trends, has sometimes been taken as evidence of convergence: but convergence can only be shown over time – and if countries start, as they do, from different positions, even similar trends (directional convergence) may not lead to increasing similarity between countries.

The evidence from the Cranet surveys shows that in Europe many aspects of HRM show directional convergence: there are similar trends. This is not always the case: the ratio of HRM specialists to the rest of the organisation, or the size of the HRM department, varies considerably with, mainly, country, but also with the size of the organisation (Brewster, 2007), but does not show any clear directional trends. Neither does training and development, which is given high priority in many countries but seems to remain the first area for cuts when finances become tight.

Despite the similarities in trends, however, there is very little evidence of countries becoming more alike in the way that they manage their human resources. The evidence is summarised as follows: from a directional convergence point of view, there seems to be a positive indication of convergence. However, when one looks at the question from a final convergence point of view, the answer is no longer a clear positive. None of the HRM practices converge (Brewster, Mayrhofer, & Morley, 2004).

Let us examine some examples of national differences: we look at communication, flexible working patterns, and the nature of the HRM department.

Communication with their workers is crucial to all organisations. Arguably, at least at the organisational level, effective communication is key to effective HRM. Yet communication varies by country. The US tends to emphasise individual communication as the key, whilst Europeans tend to stress collective communication. Because of the dominance of the US model of HRM, much of the literature associates HRM with the individualisation of communication and a move away from, or even antagonism towards, communication and consultation that is collectively or, particularly, trade union based (Brewster, 2004). But trade unionism remains widespread and important and, in Europe and elsewhere in the world, there are extensive, legally backed, systems of employee communication. These arrangements tend to supplement rather than supplant the union position (Brewster et al., 2007).

In fact, the evidence seems to show increases in all forms of communication: through representative bodies (trade unions or works councils), and through direct verbal and written communication (Brewster et al., 2007). Trade union membership remains very high in some countries (in many Nordic countries, for example, most of the workforce, including the managers, are members of trade unions); but it is much lower in some other countries and there are many where it is effectively non-existent. The increases in direct communication to employees can be explained by the development of technology: word processors and mail-merge systems allow the sending of 'individual' letters to all employees.

When upward communication is examined, the two most common means, by a considerable margin, are through immediate line management and through the trade union or works council channel. There are clear differences between countries in regard to communication design and processes. Extensive communication, both up and down seems to work: it increases most in the countries where most communication goes on (Mayrhofer, Brewster, & Morley, 2000).

Everywhere, access to financial and strategic information is clearly hierarchical. The higher your position in the organisation, the more likely you are to be regularly briefed about the financial performance of the organisation or about its strategic plans. There are noticeable differences in average 'slopes' in the distribution of this information: lower-level employees in the Nordic countries, for example, receive considerably more information than those elsewhere.

Flexibility in labour patterns is a much-discussed topic in HRM, variously referred to as 'flexibility', 'atypical working', 'vulnerable work', or 'contingent working'. Arguably, all of these terms bring with them their own metaphorical baggage. Research conducted by the Cranet network, comparing organisations at the national level across Europe (Tregaskis & Brewster, 2006), is consistent with the national labour market statistics, and workplace-level data (Kersley et al., 2006) in showing extensive use of flexible working in most developed societies, but it takes different forms in each. Temporary employment is more widespread in Europe than in the US. Part-time working is high in Denmark and short-term contracts are common in Spain. Japan has a lot of both. Differences in the kind and extent of flexible working correlate with the different institutional environments of countries (Ruiz-Quintanilla & Claes, 1996; Tregaskis & Brewster, 2006). Similarly, analyses of the extent of flexible working in Japan need to take into account the Japanese practice of restricting employment for women of above 'marriageable' age. Overall, although the trends are similar, there are still very different situations, assumptions, and practices occurring in the different countries.

However, flexible working practices are growing in both extent and coverage almost everywhere (directional convergence). This is so in nearly all countries in Europe, in Japan, and Australasia, in all parts of the economy, in organisations of all sizes, and whatever the form or origin of ownership. 'Atypical' work patterns or contracts, such as temporary, casual, fixed-term, home-based, and annual hours contracts, are spreading, despite differing legal, cultural, and labour traditions. Currently only around half of the European working population has standard (permanent, full-time, etc.) employment contracts. This has been exacerbated recently by the creation and rapid growth of the platform or 'gig' economy, where people work for (but are not employed by – they work as 'self-employed contractors') a computer-based app, so that there is no longer any personal relationship with the organisation they are working for.

All this will have extensive effects on HRM but also, beyond the world of work, in areas such as finance and the housing market (mortgages and bank loans are often dependent on 'regular' employment); tax (with people working but not paying income taxes – a major source of revenue for many countries); and demands on government resources.

The role of the HRM function, unsurprisingly, given the differences we have noted, also varies substantially across countries. Because human resources and the knowledge and skills they incorporate are difficult to replicate, they offer organisations the opportunity of obtaining sustained competitive advantage. So, we might anticipate that the influence of the human resource function on corporate decision-making increases over time. We examine the position of HRM in relation to the decision-makers within the organisation, the role of line management, and the extent of outsourcing of HRM.

In countries such as France, Spain, Sweden, and Japan, over the years 70%–80% of organisations of over 200 employees have consistently had senior HRM specialists on the company board (or its equivalent); in the Central and Eastern European countries the figures are much lower. Most European countries show that the HRM department is represented at the top decision-making level in slightly fewer than half of the organisations. When it becomes a question – perhaps the key question – of HRM influence on corporate strategy, there is more uniformity: in most countries personnel departments are involved in strategy formulation from the outset in around half of the organisations (Farndale et al., 2017).

The role of line managers in strategic (and indeed in operational) HRM has been seen as a touchstone of HRM (Darwish et al., 2017). The argument is that organisations should give more HRM responsibility to line managers who are, after all, the ones who know their people best. In fact, the trend is the other way, with most organisations centralising their HRM policies in the HRM department (Brewster, Brookes, & Gollan, 2015). Again, this varies by country and in this case largely by education standards. Countries like Finland and Denmark, with all their well-educated managers and workforces, give more responsibility to their line managers, and countries like the US and the UK, much less. These differences, too, persist over time.

Summary

Comparative HRM matters because, in each country, organisations manage their people differently. The way people are managed in the UAE is different from the way they are managed in Japan, which is different from the way they are managed in the US and so on. And although there are common trends, and there is certainly common rhetoric, there is no sign that these differences are going to decline. The best way to manage people in your country is probably very similar to the way most other people are managed; and unless you are in a very similar country to the US, the adaption of practices and policies are likely to be not only problematic but, probably, ineffective. It is important to understand the way things are done in your own country and to work from there. What is the culture of your country? What are the institutional bases (the wealth, the coherence, the legislation (and how strictly it is enforced), the education system, the labour market, etc.) of your country? Once you understand these and the typical HRM practices of your country, you will be in a much better position to decide how to improve HRM within the context that matters to you.

References

Adams, R. J., Smart, P., & Huff, A. S. (2017). Shades of grey: Guidelines for working with the grey literature in systematic reviews for management and organizational studies. *International Journal of Management Reviews*, 19, 4, 432–454.

Amable, B. (2003). *The diversity of modern capitalism*. Oxford: Oxford University Press on Demand.

Bamberger, P. (2008). Beyond contextualization: Using context theories to narrow the micro–macro gap in management research. *Academy of Management Journal*, 51, 5, 839–846.

Becker, B., & Gerhart, B. (1996). The impact of human resource management on organizational performance: Progress and prospects. *Academy of Management Journal*, 39, 4, 779–801.

Becker, B. E., & Huselid, M. A. (2006). Strategic human resources management: Where do we go from here? *Journal of Management*, 32, 6, 898–925.

Beer, M., Boselie, P., & Brewster, C. (2015). Back to the future: Implications for the field of HRM of the multistakeholder perspective proposed 30 years ago. *Human Resource Management*, 54, 3, 427–438.

Björkman, I., Fey, C. F., & Park, H. J. (2007). Institutional theory and MNC subsidiary HRM practices: Evidence from a three-country study. *Journal of International Business Studies*, 38, 3, 430–446.

Brewster, C. (1999). Strategic human resource management: The value of different paradigms. *Management International Review*, 39, 45–64.

Brewster, C. (2004). European perspectives on human resource management. *Human Resource Management Review*, 14, 4, 365–382.

Brewster, C. (2007). A European perspective on HRM. *European Journal of International Management*, 1, 3, 239–259.

Brewster, C., Brookes, M., & Gollan, P. J. (2015). The institutional antecedents of the assignment of HRM responsibilities to line managers. *Human Resource Management*, 54, 4, 577–597.

Brewster, C., Mayrhofer, W., & Farndale, E. (eds) (2018). *Handbook of research on comparative human resource management*. Chichester: Edward Elgar Publishing.

Brewster, C., Mayrhofer, W., & Morley, M. (eds) (2004). *Human resource management in Europe: Evidence of convergence?* London: Routledge.

Brewster, C., Wood, G., Croucher, C., & Brookes, M. (2007). Are works councils and joint consultative committees a threat to trade unions? A comparative analysis. *Economic and Industrial Democracy*, 28, 1, 53–81.

Cooke, F. L. (2018). Concepts, contexts, and mindsets: Putting human resource management research in perspectives. *Human Resource Management Journal*, 28, 1, 1–13.

Cooke, F. L., Veen, A., & Wood, G. (2017). What do we know about cross-country comparative studies in HRM? A critical review of literature in the period of 2000–2014. *International Journal of Human Resource Management*, 28, 1, 196–233.

Darwish, T., Mohamed, A. F., Wood, G., Singh, S., & Fleming, J. (2017). Can HRM alleviate the negative effects of the resource curse on firms? Evidence from Brunei. *Personnel Review*, 46, 8, 1931–1947.

Delery, J. E., & Doty, D. H. (1996). Modes of theorizing in strategic human resource management: Tests of universalistic, contingency, and configurational performance predictions. *Academy of Management Journal*, 394, 802–835.

Delery, J. E., & Roumpi, D. (2017). Strategic human resource management, human capital and competitive advantage: Is the field going in circles? *Human Resource Management Journal*, 27, 1, 1–21.

DiMaggio, P. J., & Powell, W. W. (1983). The iron cage revisited: Institutional isomorphism and collective rationality in organizational fields. *American Sociological Review*, 48, 147–160.

Drezner, D. W. (2001). Globalization and policy convergence. *International Studies Review*, 3, 1, 53–78.

Dunphy, D. (1987). Convergence/divergence: A temporal review of the Japanese enterprise and its management. *Academy of Management Review*, 12, 3, 445–459.

Farndale, E., Brewster, C., Ligthart, P., & Poutsma, E. (2017). The effects of market economy type and foreign MNE subsidiaries on the convergence and divergence of HRM. *Journal of International Business Studies*, 48, 9, 1065–1086.

Fenton-O'Creevy, M., & Gooderham, P. N. (2003). International management of human resources. *Scandinavian Journal of Business Research*, 17, 1, 2–5.

Fukuyama, F. (1995). Social capital and the global economy. *Foreign Affairs*, 74, 89.

Gooderham, P. N., & Brewster, C. (2003). Convergence, stasis or divergence? *Personnel Management in Europe*, Beta, 17, 1, 6–18.

Guest, D. E. (1997). Human resource management and performance: A review and research agenda. *International Journal of Human Resource Management*, 8, 3, 263–276.

Guest, D. E. (2017). Human resource management and employee well-being: Towards a new analytic framework. *Human Resource Management Journal*, 27, 1, 22–38.

Haak-Saheem, W., & Festing, M. (2016). Human resource management – A national business system perspective. *International Journal of Human Resource Management*, 1–28.

Haak-Saheem, W., Festing, M., & Darwish, T. K. (2017). International human resource management in the Arab Gulf States – An institutional perspective. *International Journal of Human Resource Management*, 28, 18, 2684–2712.

Hall, P. A., & Soskice, D. (2001). An introduction to varieties of capitalism. In P. Hall & D. Soskice (eds), *Varieties of capitalism: The institutional foundations of competitive advantage*, 1–68. Oxford: Oxford University Press.

Hofstede, G. (2001) *Culture's Consequences*, 2nd Edition. Thousand Oaks and London: Sage Publications.

Hollingsworth, J. R. (2006). A path-dependent perspective on institutional and organizational factors shaping major scientific discoveries. In J. Hage & M. Meeus (eds), *Innovation, Science, and Institutional Change*, 423–442. Oxford: Oxford University Press.

Huselid, M. A. (1995). The impact of human resource management practices on turnover, productivity, and corporate financial performance. *Academy of Management Journal*, 38, 3, 635–672.

Jackson, G., & Deeg, R. (2008). Comparing capitalisms: Understanding institutional diversity and its implications for international business. *Journal of International Business Studies*, 39, 4, 540–561.

Kersley, B., Alpin, C., Forth, J., Bryson, A., Bewley, H., Dix, G., & Oxenbridge, S. (2006). *Inside the workplace: Findings from the 2004 Workplace Employment Relations Survey*. London: Routledge.

López-Duarte, C., Vidal-Suárez, M. M., & González-Díaz, B. (2016). International business and national culture: A literature review and research agenda. *International Journal of Management Reviews*, 18, 4, 397–416.

Mayrhofer, W., Brewster, C., & Morley, M. (2000). Communication, consultation and the HRM debate. In C. Brewster, W. Mayrhofer, & M. Morley (eds), *New challenges for European human resource management*, 222–245. Basingstoke: Macmillan.

Mayrhofer, W., Brewster, C., Morley, M. J., & Ledolter, J. (2011). Hearing a different drummer? Convergence of human resource management in Europe – A longitudinal analysis. *Human Resource Management Review*, 21, 1, 50–67.

McSweeney, B. (2012). Constitutive contexts: The myths of common cultural values. In G. Wood & M. Demirbag (eds), *Handbook of institutional approaches to international business*, 142–172. Cheltenham: Edward Elgar.

Meyer, K. E. (2015). Context in management research in emerging economies. *Management and Organization Review*, 11, 3, 369–377.

Paauwe, J., & Farndale, E. (2017). *Strategy, HRM, and performance: A contextual approach*. Oxford: Oxford University Press.

Paik, Y., Vance, C. M., & Stage, H. D. (1996). The extent of divergence in human resource practice across three Chinese national cultures: Hong Kong, Taiwan and Singapore. *Human Resource Management Journal*, 6, 2, 20–31.

Pfeffer, J. (1998). Seven practices of successful organizations. *California Management Review*, 40, 2, 96–124.

Pudelko, M. (2005). Cross-national learning from best practice and the convergence–divergence debate in HRM. *International Journal of Human Resource Management*, 16, 11, 2045–2074.

Pudelko, M., & Harzing, A. W. (2007). Country-of-origin, localization, or dominance effect? An empirical investigation of HRM practices in foreign subsidiaries. *Human Resource Management*: Published in cooperation with the School of Business Administration, the University of Michigan and in alliance with the Society of Human Resources Management, 46, 4, 535–559.

Rosenzweig, P. M., & Singh, J. V. (1991). Organizational environments and the multinational enterprise. *Academy of Management Review*, 16, 2, 340–361.

Ruiz-Quintanilla, S. A., & Claes, R. (1996). Determinants of underemployment of young adults: A multicountry study. *Industrial and Labour Relations Review*, 49, 3, 424–439.

Sagiv, L., & Schwartz, S. H. (2007). Cultural values in organisations: Insights for Europe. *European Journal of International Management*, 1, 3, 176–190.

Schwartz, S. H. (1999). A theory of cultural values and some implications for work. *Applied Psychology*, 48, 1, 23–47.

Smith, C., & Meiksins, P. (1995). System, society and dominance effects in cross-national organisational analysis. *Work, Employment and Society*, 9, 2, 241–267.

Streeck, W., & Thelen, K. A. (eds) (2005). *Beyond continuity: Institutional change in advanced political economies.* Oxford: Oxford University Press.

Tregaskis, O., & Brewster, C. (2006) Converging or diverging? A comparative analysis of trends in contingent employment practice in Europe over a decade. *Journal of International Business Studies*, 37, 111–126.

Ulrich, D., Brockbank, W., & Yeung, A. (1989). Beyond belief: A benchmark for human resources. *Human Resource Management*, 28, 3, 311–335.

Uzzi, B. (1996). The sources and consequences of embeddedness for the economic performance of organizations: The network effect. *American Sociological Review*, 61, 4, 674–698.

Vaiman, V., & Brewster, C. (2015). How far do cultural differences explain the differences between nations? Implications for HRM. *International Journal of Human Resource Management*, 26, 2, 151–164.

Walker, J. T., Brewster, C., & Wood, G. (2014). Diversity between and within varieties of capitalism: Transnational survey evidence. *Industrial and Corporate Change*, 23, 2, 493–533.

Whitley, R. (1999). *Divergent capitalisms: The social structuring and change of business systems.* Oxford: Oxford University Press.

Wilkinson, A., & Wood, G. (2017). Global trends and crises, comparative capitalism and HRM. *International Journal of Human Resource Management*, 27, 18, 2503–2518.

Williamson, O. (1985). *The economic institutions of capitalism.* New York: Free Press.

Wood, G., Dibben, P., Stride, C., & Webster, E. (2011). HRM in Mozambique: Homogenization, path dependence or segmented business system? *Journal of World Business*, 46, 1, 31–41.

Wood, G., & Frynas, J. G. (2005). The institutional basis of economic failure: Anatomy of the segmented business system. *Socio-Economic Review*, 4, 2, 239–277.

Wood, G., & Lane, C. (eds) (2011). *Capitalist diversity and diversity within capitalism* (vol. 151). London: Routledge.

Wood, G., Psychogios, A., Szamosi, L. T., & Collings, D. G. (2012). Institutional approaches to comparative HRM. In C. Brewster & W. Mayrhofer (eds), *Handbook of research on comparative human resource management*, 27–50. Cheltenham: Edward Elgar.

Wright, P., & Brewster, C. (2003). Learning from diversity: HRM is not Lycra. *The International Journal of Human Resource Management*, 14, 8, 1299–1307.

Younger, J., Smallwood, N., & Ulrich, D. (2007). Developing your organization's brand as a talent developer. *People and Strategy*, 30, 2, 21.

4 International Human Resource Management

Pengiran Muda Abdul Fattaah,
Washika Haak-Saheem, Chris Brewster
and Tamer K Darwish

Introduction

A critical challenge for organisations from both the public and private sectors in the 21st century is the need to operate across national borders. The complexities of international business (IB) are no longer restricted to multinational enterprises (MNEs) but are also of concern for small- to medium-sized enterprises (SMEs) (Brewster & Scullion, 1997), international joint ventures (IJVs) (Lu & Björkman, 1997), and not-for-profit organisations. It has long been highlighted that in international organisations human resources are a critical source of competitive advantage (Schuler, Dowling, & De Cieri, 1993; Caligiuri & Stroh, 1995; Minbaeva, 2018). Since its early beginnings, there has been both an evolution of territory covered by the international human resource management (IHRM) field and a more critical discussion of whether this evolution has been towards an expanded field or represents a process of fragmentation.

Globalisation is key to understanding the changing nature of business at the level of industry, firm, and function. Thus, globalisation has been seen as a direct factor influencing firms' levels of international trade, intensity of international competition, product standardisation, presence of international competitors in geographic markets, cost drivers, and location of value-adding activities (Johansson & Yip, 1994). Firm-level globalisation studies consider factors such as foreign subsidiary sales, export sales, level of foreign assets, number of foreign subsidiaries, and level and dispersion of top managers' international experience (Ramaswamy, Kroeck, & Renforth, 1996). Functional-level globalisation studies concentrate on different mechanisms of people, information, formalisation- or centralisation-based integration, organisational design features, and attitudinal orientations (Kim & Gray, 2005). The changes in how international operating companies have been managed in recent decades have implications for their HRM policies and practices.

So, this chapter explains and discusses the concepts and theories behind human resource management (HRM) and IHRM, as well as exploring the various concepts that may affect the ways HRM is utilised by MNEs. Additionally, we review and critically discuss the theoretical and empirical work that has been carried out to explain the differences in HRM in domestic organisations and MNEs, highlighting the importance of understanding these differences when looking at the relationship between HRM and performance. Despite a wealth of existing literature, the field of IHRM is changing rapidly and, arguably, theorisation has not kept up with developments in practice.

The International Dimension of HRM

The point of HRM is that human beings working for an organisation are considered valuable assets who need to be handled efficiently and effectively in order to maximise returns from these assets (Collings, Wood, & Szamosi, 2009). Much of the scholarly discussion has turned on how that is interpreted (maximum returns for whose benefit?) (Beer, Boselie, & Brewster, 2015) and how it is done; hence, it might be argued that a widely accepted definition of HRM is yet to be formed (Guest, 1997; Paauwe & Boselie, 2005; Darwish, Singh, & Wood, 2015), and the definitions of HRM given by the various scholars differ depending on their approach and areas of interest.

Historically, the concept of HRM as a management science originated in the US in the 1960s and was further developed in the 1970s and early 1980s by changes in organisational planning and approaches towards employees. The shift towards the use of HRM to define people management can be seen to have started in the late 1980s. Since the introduction of HRM as a required subject on the MBA programme by the Harvard Business School in 1981, the concept has attained ever greater levels of visibility (Keenoy, 1990; Poole, 1990). This has reflected a growth in the use of 'HRM' in enterprises and, alongside the rapidly changing environment in which such enterprises operate, the concept is constantly evolving to keep up with the more complex needs.

Two prominent concepts have been used to develop the initial concept of HRM: strategic human resource management (SHRM) and IHRM. In so far as the concept of HRM sees people as valued resources in who companies should invest in order to improve current performance and ensure future growth, Guest (1989) argues that SHRM is the integration of HRM policies into strategic planning, to ensure the coherence of HRM policies as applied by line managers in their everyday work. This is echoed in a definition of SHRM offered by Wright and McMahan (1992) where SHRM is the pattern of planned HRM deployments and activities envisioned to support the organisation to achieve its goals. Wright and Snell (1991) and Ulrich and Lake (1991) see the concept as the design of systems to ensure that people can be a sustainable source of competitive advantage linking both HRM practices and business strategy.

IHRM emerged from the growth of IB and the increase in the number of companies doing business outside of their home countries. IHRM in such firms was again argued to be a key success factor. For many MNEs, as for most other businesses, the cost of their human resources is the largest single item of their operating costs. The knowledge and capabilities incorporated in a firm's human resources are critical to the business performance. Thus, HRM has been considered a key determinant of the competitiveness of the firm. For firms operating internationally, the level of complexity increases with the degree of IB activities, and so does their HRM.

The international orientation of the firm requires the active support of HRM policies and practices. The economic integration of the 21st century, the reduction of barriers to labour mobility across the globe, and the development of new technologies have encouraged companies to establish international operations. Nor is this trend confined to the private sector. Governments and internationally operating non-government organisations (NGOs) need to manage their employees around the world. For example, international organisations such as the United Nations (UN) or the Gulf Cooperation Council (GCC) states are heavily engaged in activities across national borders (Brewster & Lee, 2006).

Nonetheless, most work in HRM, and most research in IHRM, in particular (Kaufmann, 2016), has taken place amongst private sector companies and has been carried out in the WEIRD – Western, educated, industrialised, rich, democratic – countries (Henrich, Heine, & Norenzayan, 2010). The context in this stream of IHRM is reflected in an over-representation of studies looking at Western developed-country MNEs transferring HRM practices to non-Western developing host-country settings. Studies on developing-country MNEs are also under-represented, although they have been increasing (e.g., Cooke, Wood, & Horwitz, 2015; Tatoglu, Glaister, & Demirbag, 2016; Haak-Saheem, Festing, & Darwish, 2017).

Global Mobility

For many people, IHRM is more or less synonymous with expatriation: the transfer by MNEs of their employees around the world to the different parts of their business. Expatriates are people working legally in another country for a limited period of time (McNulty & Brewster, 2017). Expatriation takes many forms. Most of the research has been done on long-term expatriates assigned and transferred by their employers (AEs). Research on AEs has been at the centre of academic attention for decades (Edström & Galbraith, 1977; Black, Mendenhall, & Oddou, 1991; Brewster & Scullion, 1997) and the number of AEs is increasing over time. Research has examined a wide range of factors about such expatriates: demographics, personality, gender, and location;

remuneration, benefits, tax, and social security issues; legal and labour law concerns; motivations to go, selection, training and development, adjustment, family concerns, health and well-being, repatriation and retention and subsequent careers; hostile environments, host teams, and the wider host-country context; and performance (McNulty & Brewster, 2019).

Organisations send employees on their international assignments to control the MNEs' foreign subsidiaries, to provide expertise lacking in the subsidiary or to develop (and test) their potential global leaders (Edström & Galbraith, 1977). Such expatriates are extremely costly for the MNEs and their management requires considerable attention, meaning they continue to be the main subject of international mobility research (McNulty & Brewster, 2019). However, some of the objectives can be reached in whole or in part through other forms of mobility, and attention has more recently been directed to them. These include the following:

- *Short-term expatriates*: people who are sent usually for less than six months and whose families do not relocate with them.
- *Self-initiated expatriates:* people who are not sent by their employer but make their own way to another county and then take up work there, including the largest group of expatriates: low-status expatriates (Haak-Saheem & Brewster, 2017).
- *Migrants:* people who may be highly skilled or less skilled but who intend to settle in their new country and to live and work there for the foreseeable future; including a group of people who have been forced out of their own country and are generally called 'refugees'.
- *Frequent travellers, month-on-month-off, and commuters:* people whose work may take them internationally but only for brief periods, and whose families stay at home.

However, not all IHRM is about international mobility. IB scholars do not always ask the same questions of people management in international organisations as scholars do of indigenous organisations. They tend to have their own perspective and views. However, it is important to HRM researchers and practitioners to understand the IB perspectives as they inform our IHRM approach. There are debates in the literature that are of relevance to the field of IB.

Globalisation

Globalisation increased in importance throughout the late 20th century and, albeit unevenly, in the 21st century. It is an ambiguous concept whose impact has been subject to much debate and it is defined by scholars differently depending on their field. Scholars such as Todaro (1997) see it as the process through which the world increasingly functions as a single community rather than as many widely separated communities. A certain ambiguity arises from the lack of a precise definition and this is highlighted in the way some authors have used globalisation interchangeably with similar concepts such as internationalisation and Westernisation. The situation is not helped by the many aspects of globalisation, which can range from political and economic aspects to sociological perspectives. Scholte (2000) observes a range of eight different themes that summarise the areas where globalisation can occur:

- Global communications, including transportation and telecommunications
- Global markets, including products, services, and organisational strategies
- Global production, including production chains and collections of resources
- Global money, including currencies and credit cards
- Global finance, including banking and foreign exchange markets
- Global organisations, including NGOs and MNEs
- Global social ecology, including the atmosphere and geosphere
- Global consciousness, where the world is seen as a single place and communities are closer

In an economic context, globalisation can be seen as the process through which consumer markets, production lines, labour, technology, and investments are viewed as more internationally integrated (Held et al., 1999; Lall, 1999). As a result of globalisation, organisations compete on a global scale rather than just focusing on regional markets, as was previously favoured (Bartlett & Ghoshal, 1998). It must be noted, however, that the majority of MNEs should and do compete strategically on a regional or even local basis (Rugman, 2003; Ghemawat, 2005; Greenwald & Kahn, 2005). Furthermore, authors such as Prahalad (1976), Doz (1979) and Bartlett and Ghoshal (1998) have stressed the importance of national responsiveness, which takes into account the fact that customers in different markets do not have identical tastes, and it is strategically advantageous to adapt products tailored to local demand.

This places new burdens on firms and organisations seeking to improve their competitiveness. As competition in their economic arenas increases, their ability to set prices decreases and this leads to situations where their profitability is increasingly dependent on their ability to cut the costs of inputs, as well as enhancing their productivity. MNEs, which operate across national boundaries, are most susceptible to the forces of globalisation and are therefore more likely to implement more dominant global practices to enhance their competitiveness in the foreign markets in which they operate.

Country of Origin

Research in the area of business systems has suggested that home country institutions heavily influence an MNE's behaviour and structure. For example, the level at which the MNE is embedded in the home country affects the transfer of operational modes, competencies, and frameworks, as they are developed there. This is important as the transfer of these developments to subsidiaries in the different host countries will need to take into account the level of organisational structures there as well as the level at which the country of origin needs to be mediated.

Internationalisation strategies are employed by multinationals when headquarters handle subsidiaries and the different markets and situations where they operate. Following Bartlett and Ghoshal (1998), the main dimensions of internationalisation strategies involve 'global integration', which refers to the interdependence of subsidiaries and headquarters and the need to cater to local markets and other situational specificities. Corporate control basically has two dimensions: the directness and explicitness of control, and the impersonality of control (see March & Simon, 1958; Lawrence & Lorsch, 1967; Child, 1973, 1984; Galbraith, 1973; Mintzberg, 1979, 1983; Hennart, 1991).

Many MNEs do not aim to be globally integrated, preferring to take advantage of the differences between countries (Rugman & Verbeke, 2001), but those that do have been the subject of attention of most work in IHRM. Such organisations need to be both 'globally integrated' and 'locally responsive', perhaps aiming to appear less clearly tied to a single context of origin as they may share ownership and utilise diverse human and capital resources. However, the style of HRM transfer very much depends on the country of origin itself, as can be seen from the ratio of invested capital and human resources inside the country of origin to those outside. Even early in this century, of the world's top ten multinationals, only two were North American enterprises, and the rest were European (Dowling & Welch, 2004). This is of course partly because the North American home market is so big that having a large proportion of business outside the home country is more difficult for them than for MNEs from smaller countries. Bartlett and Ghoshal (1998) found that European MNEs have high local responsiveness and low interdependence, whilst Japanese MNEs had the opposite. American MNEs fell between these two extremes.

Method of Establishment

The transfer of HRM from the headquarters to a subsidiary can be an important indicator of the level of control held by the headquarters over the subsidiary. However, the MNE's ability to control its subsidiaries can also be affected by the ownership structure of the MNE or the level of ownership held in a particular subsidiary. The level of control exerted by the parent company is reflected in its choice of whether to have 'high control', which occurs in wholly owned subsidiaries, or 'low control', which happens in joint ventures in foreign markets (Kogut & Singh, 1988; Agarwal, 1994). The need for greater control over wholly owned subsidiaries than over IJVs is strongly related to the degree of resources committed to each. Higher levels of control would mean the subsidiary adhering more closely to the MNE's standard of HRM practices rather than following those of DEs. The limited evidence we have is that MNEs tend to adopt hybrid practices – some amalgam of headquarters' practices and local practice (Chung, Sparrow, & Bozkurt, 2014), and that they operate differently from indigenous companies, but not that differently (Farndale, Brewster, & Poutsma, 2008). Given the need to follow local laws and to operate in accordance with local expectations, that may not be too surprising.

Organisational Culture

The issue of culture is not new. It was explored as early as the 1930s and its prominence has increased due to the works of Hofstede (1980), who argues that culture is the collective programming of a group that shares the same beliefs, assumptions, and norms. Values, as defined by Hofstede (2001), are a broad tendency to prefer certain states of affairs over others and are normally formed by social interactions in the early years of an individual's life. It is because of the importance placed on these values that many scholars have emphasised differences in culture as an increasingly important variable when looking at management, including HRM. These scholars believe that there are no universal solutions when it comes to solving problems that arise in management due to culture. Hofstede (2001) instead proposes distinct 'national economic cultures', which divide countries along an axis of his famous five (earlier four cultural dimensions: hierarchy, individualism, uncertainty avoidance, masculinity, and long-term orientation.

In general, due to the nature of their international engagement and activities, MNEs face more competitive environments than DEs. The threat of competition arises from DEs, as well as from the affiliates of fellow MNEs, who often follow their rivals overseas to protect their markets (Porter, 1986). In order to remain competitive, MNEs, it is argued, are always looking to excel in their operations to enhance their competitive advantage and, accordingly, to stay ahead of the competition. As a result, on issues of central importance, such as HRM, MNEs take a much more methodical and structured approach which, *a priori*, can be argued to be more rigorous than those in the local environment. Therefore, all MNEs need to be concerned, on an operational basis, with HRM issues on an international or global platform (Sparrow & Brewster, 2006).

Previous research argues that HRM practices may differ across different countries because of certain tendencies that can be found in their laws and policies and the multiple cultures that may be inherent in them (Hofstede, 1993; Ferner, 1997; Zhang, 2003). Conflicts may occur when the parent and subsidiary face different and sometimes contradictory economic, social, and political systems in the countries where they operate. Some parent enterprises will insist on pushing policies that reflect their own corporate culture (Rosenzweig & Singh, 1991), but these may be constrained by the host-country environment, requiring these foreign enterprises to conform to local management practices and policies rather than implementing their global strategies.

There are many examples of the wholesale adoption of parent company practices being seen as disadvantageous and inappropriate due to the differences between the cultures of the home and host countries (Trompennars, 1993; Shenkar & Von Glinlow, 1994; Cascio & Bailey, 1995). Therefore, subsidiaries of MNEs are faced with dual pressures: whether to be consistent with the rest of the MNE or to conform to the local environment (Hedlund, 1986; Porter, 1986; Rosenzweig & Singh, 1991; Bartlett & Ghoshal, 1998). It has also been seen that the cultures inherent in a society may influence how the different HRM practices are implemented in those countries (Chung, Sparrow, & Bozkurt, 2014).

However, there are criticisms of the cultural approach. Scholars such as Rowley and Lewis (1996) see national cultures as complex systems that make the separation and comparison of the different cultural attributes difficult and dangerous. The cultural approach also emphasises history and individual perceptions whilst forgetting that these may change over time, as generations pass. Values on their own are insufficient as it is necessary to look at the societal and economic structures of a society (Evans & Lorange, 1989; Whitehill, 1991; Vaiman & Brewster, 2015).

International HRM

The concept of IHRM has followed a significant trend during the past quarter of a century, especially in North America (Schuler, 2000; Reynolds, 2001; Briscoe & Schuler, 2004; Schuler & Jackson, 2005; Stahl & Björkman, 2006). Early research on IB assumed that there would be ever more common global organisational practices, or isomorphism, and that this would apply to HRM too (Kidger, 2002). The focus of this research was on the particular advantages that firms gain from operating internationally. There was a general understanding that MNEs would impose change on the host country – moving it towards the US, 'best practice', model. Hence, firms were expected to focus on the standardisation side of the standardisation/differentiation dilemma (Ashkenas et al., 1995). Pressures to comply to local norms are seen as a limitation to be overcome and firms operate 'guided by unambiguous preferences' for standardisation and with 'bounded rationality' (Gooderham, Nordhaug, & Ringdal, 1999: 507). In a similar vein, research on IHRM assumes that MNCs tend to gain international advantage by diffusing what they see as the most efficient ways of handling HRM (normally the way it is done at head offices) in international locations (Myloni, Harzing, & Mirza, 2007).

Accordingly, practitioners and scholars often consider the standardisation of HRM practices as a winning strategy across the globe (Sparrow, Brewster, & Harris, 2004). However, if internationally operating firms apply standard policies in different contexts, they will either spread modern practices around the world, reducing their competitive advantage, or it will mean that they are applying inappropriate policies that will not achieve what they are looking for.

Policies are often standardised, but there is a lot of evidence that practices are not. The literature is beginning to develop and investigate the argument that there is a distinction between HRM policies (set by the head office HRM experts) and HRM practices (utilised by managers dealing with the employees in their foreign subsidiaries) (Nishii et al., 2018). In other words, even in the most centralised MNE there is a considerable variation in actual practices. Generally speaking, policies are in fact subject to a wide range of different responses from local managers and employees (Oliver, 1991). HRM policies get either explicitly or more often implicitly negotiated or varied at a national level (Ferner, 1997; Chung, Sparrow, & Bozkurt, 2014). HRM is highly contextual (Baron & Kreps, 1999).

Summary

We have seen that the literature on comparative HRM considers the differences in HRM in different countries (Brewster, Mayrhofer, & Morley, 2004). These issues are covered in more detail in the chapter on comparative HRM, but clearly, these international differences mean that managing HRM across many countries will be different from managing HRM in only one country. Moreover, IHRM has been considered to have the same main dimensions as HRM in a national context but to operate on a larger scale, with more complex strategic considerations, more complex coordination and control demands, and some additional HRM functions (Engle, Dowling, & Festing, 2008). Hence, HRM in internationally operating firms has to accommodate the need for greater operating unit diversity, more external stakeholder influence, higher levels of risk exposure, and more personal insight into employees' lives and family situation (Tarique & Schuler, 2010). The research focused on understanding those HRM functions changes as firms go international. The literature has also begun to identify important contingencies that influenced how certain HRM functions were internationalised; into which countries, the size and life cycle stage of the firm, types of employee, etc. (Aycan, 2005).

The literature on IHRM has broadened its focus from a narrow view on the practical issues raised by relocating people around the world to more ambitious attempts to understand the strategic value of HR policies and practices within international organisations. Thus, the field has expanded from a focus on the management of expatriates (Tung, 1982; Mendenhall & Oddou, 1985) into a growing literature on IB strategy (Porter, 1996; Bartlett & Ghoshal, 1998), examining issues of managing people in international organisations.

Clearly, the field of IHRM has become substantially more important in every way because of globalisation. It deals with the movement of information and knowledge, as well as people and services, across borders, facilitated and accelerated by changes in every environment, from the economic and political to the social and cultural, as well as any advances in the technological and legal arenas. It is the characteristics of these conditions that are important for MNEs and IHRM. IHRM has its roots in the research conducted on MNEs and their tendency to utilise expatriates in subsidiaries, as well as the selection, training, and management of these employees (Dowling & Welch, 2004). And although expatriates remain an important part of MNEs' operations overseas, the scope of research has broadened from long-term expatriation to take into account the increasing portfolio of activities that an MNE could be involved in outside its home country.

There are other critical mechanisms that can be seen to affect coordination and control in MNEs. Organisations may choose many different paths in order to achieve the same results (Hendry & Pettigrew, 1992), as there are many linkages between the external environment, which includes the legal, socio-economic, political, technological and competitive environments, and the internal organisational culture, which includes organisational structure, leadership styles, technology, and business output (Budhwar & Debrah, 2001). Therefore, understanding the relationships between firms' international strategies and IHRM policies and practices is critical for their international competitiveness.

References

Agarwal, S. (1994). Socio-cultural distance and the choice of joint ventures: A contingency perspective. *Journal of International Marketing*, 2, 2, 63–80.

Ashkenas, R., Ulrich, D., Jick, T., & Kerr, S. (1995). *The boundaryless organization*. San Francisco, CA: Jossey-Bass.

Aycan, Z. (2005). The interplay between cultural and institutional/structural contingencies in human resource management practices. *International Journal of Human Resource Management*, 16, 1083–1119.

Baron, J. N., & Kreps, D. M. (1999). Consistent human resource practices. *California Management Review*, 41, 3, 29–53.

Bartlett, C. A., & Ghoshal, S. (1998). *Managing across borders: The transnational solution* (2nd edn). Boston, MA: Harvard Business School Press.

Beer, M., Boselie, P., & Brewster, C. (2015). Back to the future: Implications for the field of HRM of the multi-stakeholder perspective proposed 30 years ago. *Human Resource Management*, 54, 3, 427–438.

Black, J. S., Mendenhall, M., & Oddou, G. (1991). Toward a comprehensive model of international adjustment: An integration of multiple theoretical perspectives. *Academy of Management Review*, 16, 2, 291–317.

Brewster, C., & Lee, S. (2006). HRM in not-for-profit international organizations: Different, but also alike. In H. H. Larsen & W. Mayrhofer (eds), *European Human Resource Management*, 131–148. London: Routledge.

Brewster, C., Mayrhofer, W., & Morley, M. (Eds.). (2004). *Human resource management in Europe: Evidence of convergence?* London: Routledge.

Brewster, C., & Scullion, H. (1997). A review and agenda for expatriate HRM. *Human Resource Management Journal*, 7, 3, 32–41.

Briscoe, D., & Schuler, R. (2004). *International human resource management: Policies & practices for the global enterprise* (2nd edn). New York: Routledge.

Budhwar, P., & Debrah, Y. (2001). Rethinking comparative and cross national human resource management research. *International Journal of Human Resource Management*, 12, 3, 497–515.

Caligiuri, P. M., & Stroh, L. K. (1995). Multinational corporation management strategies and international human resources practices: Bringing IHRM to the bottom line. *International Journal of Human Resource Management*, 6, 3, 494–507.

Cascio, W., & Bailey, E. (1995). *International human resource management: The state of research and practices in global perspectives of human resource management*. Englewood Cliffs, NJ: Prentice Hall.

Child, J. (1973). Strategies of control and organization behavior. *Administrative Science Quarterly*, 18, 1–17.

Child, J. (1984). *Organisation: A guide to problems and practice* (2nd edn). London: Paul Chapman.

Chung, C., Sparrow, P., & Bozkurt, Ö. (2014). South Korean MNEs' international HRM approach: Hybridization of global standards and local practices. *Journal of World Business*. 49, 4, 549–559.

Collings, D. G., Wood, G. T., & Szamosi, L. T. (2009). Human resource management: A critical approach. In *Human Resource Management*. London: Routledge, pp. 1–24.

Cooke, F. L., Wood, G., & Horwitz, F. (2015). Multinational firms from emerging economies in Africa: Implications for research and practice in human resource management. *International Journal of Human Resource Management*, 26, 21, 2653–2675.

Darwish, T., Singh, S., & Wood, G. (2015). The impact of human resource practices on actual and perceived organizational performance in a Middle-Eastern emerging market. *Human Resource Management*, 55, 2, 261–281.

Dowling, P. J., & Welch, D. E. (2004). *International human resource management: Managing people in a multinational context* (4th edn). London: Thomson.

Doz, Y. L. (1979). *Government control and multinational strategic management: Power systems and telecommunication equipment*. New York: Praeger.

Edström, A., & Galbraith, J. R. (1977). Transfer of managers as a coordination and control strategy in multinational organizations. *Administrative Science Quarterly*, 22, 2, 248–263.

Engle, A. D., Dowling, P. J., & Festing, M. (2008). State of origin: Research in global performance management, a proposed research domain, and emerging implications. *European Journal of International Management*, 2, 153–169.

Evans, P., & Lorange, P. (1989). The two logics behind human resource management. In P. Evans, Y. Doz, & A. Laurent (eds), *Human resource management in international firms. Change, globalization, innovation*. London: Macmillan.

Farndale, E., Brewster, C., & Poutsma, E. (2008). Coordinated vs. liberal market HRM: the impact of institutionalization on multinational firms. *International Journal of Human Resource Management*, 19, 11, 2004–2023.

Ferner, A. (1997). Country of origin effects and HRM in multinational companies. *Human Resource Management Journal*, 7, 1, 19–37.

Galbraith, J. R. (1973). *Designing complex organizations*. Reading, MA: Addison.

Ghemawat, P. (2005 December). Regional strategies for global leadership. *Harvard Business Review*, 83, 12, 98–108.

Gooderham, P. N., Nordhaug, O., & Ringdal, K. (1999). Institutional and rational determinants of organizational practices: Human resource management in European firms. *Administrative Science Quarterly*, 44, 3, 507–531.

Greenwald, B., & Kahn, J. (2005 September). All strategy is local. *Harvard Business Review*, 83, 95–104.

Guest, D. E. (1989 January). Personnel and HRM: Can you tell the difference? *Personnel Management*, 21, 48–51.

Guest, D. E. (1997). Human resource management and performance: A review and research agenda. *International Journal of Human Resource Management*, 8, 3, 263–276.

Haak-Saheem, W., & Brewster, C. (2017). Hidden expatriates: International mobility in the United Arab Emirates as a challenge to current understanding of expatriation. *Human Resource Management Journal*, 27, 3, 423–439.

Haak-Saheem, W., Festing, M., & Darwish, T. K. (2017). International human resource management in the Arab Gulf States – an institutional perspective. *International Journal of Human Resource Management*, 28, 18, 2684–2712.

Hedlund, G. (1986). The hypermodern MNC: A heterarchy? *Human Resource Management*, 25, 9–35.

Held, D., McGrew, A., Goldblatt, D., & Perraton, J. (1999). *Global transformations: Politics, economics and culture*. Cambridge: Polity Press.

Hendry, C., & Pettigrew, A. M. (1992). Patterns of strategic change in the development of human resource management. *British Journal of Management*, 3, 137–156.

Hennart, J. F. (1991). Control in multinational firms: The role of price and hierarchy. *Management International Review*, 31, 71–96.

Henrich, J., Heine, S. J., & Norenzayan, A. (2010). The weirdest people in the world? *Behavioral and Brain Sciences*, 33, (2–3), 61–83.

Hofstede, G. (1980). *Culture's consequences: International differences in work-related values*. Beverly Hills, CA: SAGE.

Hofstede, G. (1993). Intercultural conflict and synergy in Europe. In D. J. Hickson (ed.), *Management in Western Europe: Society, culture and organization in twelve nations*, 1–8. Berlin: Walter de Gruyter.

Hofstede, G. (2001). *Culture's consequences: Comparing values, behaviours, institutions, and organizations across nations.* Thousand Oaks, CA: SAGE.

Johansson, J., & Yip, G. (1994). Exploiting globalization potential: US and Japanese strategies. *Strategic Management Journal*, 15, 8, 579–601.

Kaufman, B. E. (2016). Globalization and convergence–divergence of HRM across nations: New measures, explanatory theory, and non-standard predictions from bringing in economics. *Human Resource Management Review*, 26, 4, 338–351.

Keenoy, T. (1990). HRM: A case of the wolf in sheep's clothing? *Personnel Review*, 19, 2, 3–9.

Kidger, P. J. (2002). Management structure in multinational enterprises: Responding to globalization. *Employee Relations*, 24, 1, 69–85.

Kim, Y., & Gray, S. J. (2005). Strategic factors influencing international human resource management practices: An empirical study of Australian multinational corporations. *International Journal of Human Resource Management*, 16, 5, 809–830.

Kogut, B., & Singh, H. (1988). The effect of national culture on the choice of entry mode. *Journal of International Business Studies*, 19, 3, 411–432.

Lall, R. (1999). Rethinking Asia: Time to get wired. *Far Easter Economic Review*, August 19.

Lawrence, J. W., & Lorsch, P. R. (1967). *Organizations and environments.* Cambridge, MA: Harvard University Press.

Lu, Y., & Björkman, I. (1997). HRM practices in China–Western joint ventures: MNC standardization versus localization. *International Journal of Human Resource Management*, 8, 614–628.

March, J. G., & Simon, H. A. (1958). *Organizations.* New York: Wiley.

McNulty, Y., & Brewster, C. (2017). Theorizing the meaning(s) of 'expatriate': Establishing boundary conditions for business expatriates. *International Journal of Human Resource Management*, 28, 1, 27–61.

McNulty, Y., & Brewster, C. (2019). *Working internationally: Expatriation, migration and other global work.* Cheltenham: Edward Elgar.

Mendenhall, M., & Oddou, G. (1985). The dimensions of expatriate acculturation: A review. *Academy of Management Review*, 10, 1, 39–47.

Minbaeva, D. B. (2018). Building credible human capital analytics for organizational competitive advantage. *Human Resource Management*, 57, 3, 701–713.

Mintzberg, H. (1979). *The structuring of organizations.* Englewood Cliffs, NJ: Prentice Hall.

Mintzberg, H. (1983). *Power in and around organisations.* Englewood Cliffs NJ: Prentice Hall.

Myloni, B., Harzing, A. W., & Mirza, H. (2007). The effect of corporate-level organizational factors on the transfer of human resource management practices: European and US MNCs and their Greek subsidiaries. *International Journal of Human Resource Management*, 18, 12, 2057–2074.

Nishii, L. H., Khattab, J., Shemla, M., & Paluch, R. M. (2018). A multi-level process model for understanding diversity practice effectiveness. *Academy of Management Annals*, 12, 37–82. doi:10.5465/annals.2016.0044

Oliver, C. (1991). Strategic responses to institutional processes. *Academy of Management Review*, 16, 145–179.

Paauwe, J., & Boselie, P. (2005). HRM and performance: What next? *Human Resource Management Journal*, 15, 4, 68–83.

Poole, M. (1990). Editorial: Human resource management in an international perspective. *International Journal of Human Resource Management*, 1, 1–15.

Porter, M. E. (1986). Competition in global industries: A conceptual framework. In M. Porter, (ed.), *Competition in Global Industries*, 15–60. Boston, MA: Harvard Business School Press.

Prahalad, C. K. (1976). Strategic choices in diversified MNCs. *Harvard Business Review*, 54, 4, 67–78.

Ramaswamy, K., Kroeck, K. G., & Renforth, W. (1996). Measuring the degree of internationalization of a firm: A comment. *Journal of International Business Studies*, 27, 1, 167–177.

Reynolds, C. (2001). Compensation and benefits in a global context. In C. Reynolds (ed.), *Guide to global compensation and benefits*. San Diego, CA: Harcourt.

Rosenzweig, P. M., & Singh, J. V. (1991). Organizational environments and the multinational enterprise. *Academy of Management Review*, 16, 2, 340–361.

Rowley, C., & Lewis, M. (1996). Greater China at the crossroads: Convergence, culture and competitiveness. *Asia Pacific Business Review*, 2, 3, 1–22.

Rugman, A. (2003). Regional strategy and the demise of globalization. *Journal of International Management*, 9, 409–417.

Rugman, A., & Verbeke, A. (2001). Subsidiary-specific advantages in multinational enterprises. *Strategic Management Journal*, 22, 3, 237–250.

Scholte, J. A. (2000). *Globalisation: A critical introduction*. London: Macmillan.

Schuler, R. S. (2000). The internationalization of human resource management. *Journal of International Management*, 6, 239–260.

Schuler, R. S., Dowling, P. J., & De Cieri, H. (1993). An integrative framework of strategic international human resource management. *Journal of Management*, 19, 2, 419–459.

Schuler, R. S., & Jackson, S. E. (2005). A quarter-century review of human resource management in the US: The growth in importance of the international perspective. *Management Review*, 16, 11–35.

Shenkar, O., & Von Glinow, M. A. (1994). Paradoxes of organizational theory and research: Using the case of China to illustrate national contingency. *Management Science*, 40, 1, 56–71.

Sparrow, P., Brewster, C., & Harris, H. (2004). *Globalizing human resource management*. London; New York: Routledge.

Sparrow, P. R., & Brewster, C. (2006). Globalizing HRM: The growing revolution in managing employees internationally. In C. Cooper and R. Burke (eds), *The human resources revolution: Research and practice*. London: Elsevier, pp. 99–122.

Stahl, G. K., & Björkman, I. (2006). *Handbook of research in international human resource management*. Cheltenham: Edward Elgar.

Tarique, I., & Schuler, R. S. (2010). Global talent management: Literature review, integrative framework, and suggestions for further research. *Journal of World Business*, 45, 2, 122–133.

Tatoglu, E., Glaister, A. J., & Demirbag, M. (2016). Talent management motives and practices in an emerging market: A comparison between MNEs and local firms. *Journal of World Business*, 51, 2, 278–293.

Todaro, M. (1997). *Economic development* (6th edn). Essex: Addison Wesley Longman Limited.

Trompennars, F. (1993). *Riding the waves of culture: Understanding cultural diversity in business*. London: Nicholas Brealey Publishing.

Tung, R. (1982). Selection and training procedures of US, European and Japanese multinationals. *California Management Review*, 25, 57–71.

Ulrich, D., & Lake, D. (1991). Organizational capability: Creating competitive advantage. *Academy of Management Executive*, 5, 1, 77–92.

Vaiman, V., & Brewster, C. (2015). How far do cultural differences explain the differences between nations? Implications for HRM. *International Journal of Human Resource Management*, 26, 2, 151–164.

Whitehill, A. (1991). *Japanese management*. London: Routledge.

Wright, P. M., & McMahan, G. C. (1992). Theoretical perspectives for strategic human resource management. *Journal of Management*, 18, 2, 295–321.

Wright, P. M., & Snell, S. A. (1991). Toward an integrative view of strategic human resource management. *Human Resource Management Review*, 1, 3, 203–225.

Zhang, M. (2003). Transferring human resource management across national boundaries: The case of Chinese multinational companies in the UK. *Employee Relations*, 25, 6, 613–627.

5 Institutions, Complementarity, Human Resource Management, and Performance

Satwinder Singh, Tamer K Darwish, Geoffrey Wood, and Pengiran Muda Abdul Fattaah

Introduction

This chapter presents an examination of organisations, and the rate and overall use of more professional and well-considered HR practices in what is recognised as being a market environment, where there may be a lesser degree of fluidity and development in terms of national institutional arrangements (Singh et al., 2017). Emphasis is placed, in this chapter, on Brunei, which is a petro-state located in South-East Asia. The literature available with regard to within-capitalism diversity posits the view that, when there is a greater degree of fluidity or arguable weakness across national-level institutions, there will be a lack of consistency in regulatory coverage, with key sub-national institutional arrangements then recognised as being more advantageous with regard to the requirements of particular categories of actors as opposed to others (Wood and Lane, 2012). Once again, the literature available on the commonly labelled resource curse implies that revenues created as a result of resource windfall, as is recognised in the instance of petro-states, can be responsible for the government failing to invest in institution-building, as highlighted in the study by Auty (2002); it is notable to highlight that economic development can be achieved even when there is a lack of alignment or complete functionality in terms of institutional arrangements (Singh et al., 2017). Subsequently, this could be responsible for the significant variation recognised from one sector to the next (Rugman & Oh, 2013; Nguyen, 2014), with a greater degree of contribution and value offered by HR practices, meaning they are then well positioned to flourish in some arenas but not in others. Taking this into account, we aim to investigate the numerous recognised differences in the effectiveness of HR practices in line with sector and size, enabling specific attention to be directed towards the differences between the gas and oil industry, in addition to other fields in the economy. There is also the view that performance is improved upon and expanded when HR practices are presented in a bundle or otherwise through a synergetic system, with practices used in isolation believed to achieve lesser outcomes in terms of performance than if numerous were to be used together (Ichniowski &

Shaw, 1999). It may be posited that this highlights the foundational nature of complementarity across specific institutional environments (Hall & Soskice, 2001). In particular, the literature available on comparative capitalism implies that, in those institutional contexts that are not as well developed, it is unlikely that practices and regulations will demonstrate complementarities, which accordingly means that similarly mutually supportive practices are less likely to be more proficient than interventions used individually with the aim of overcoming business obstacles (Hall & Soskice, 2001; Hancke et al., 2007; Singh et al., 2019). Nonetheless, a number of different players in the field may design their own potential approaches for specific organisations, either through establishing ways around formal regulations or otherwise by creating and implementing more informal micro-regulatory solutions, in line with their own specific skillsets, position and abilities (Wood et al., 2011).

The Context of Brunei

The economy of Brunei is recognised as having been dominated by liquefied natural gas and oil industries following on from their initial discovery during the early 1960s (Singh et al., 2017). The literature available that has been published on the so-called resource curse is abundant and emphasises the extent to which resource-rich countries commonly find themselves with a lack of industry in other areas besides the natural resource, with economic activity across other areas seen to be lacking any competitive edge (Heeks, 1998; Auty, 2002; Darwish et al., 2017). It is recognised that there is the potential for overvalued currency to stem from gas and oil exports, which then means other exports become too costly (Singh et al., 2017). The advantages and opportunities presented by the oil and gas sector could also mean investment in other fields is crowded out, meaning those sectors of capital not falling in the resources group are then starved of investment, with the government also directing their funds elsewhere (Auty, 2002). When examining those countries that are seen to be rich in natural resources, revenues flow to a significant degree, irrespective of organisations' functionality. Subsequently, this causes incentives surrounding the expansion and development of institutions to decrease (Singh et al., 2017). Once again, owing to the fact that there is a significant degree of volatility identifiable across commodity markets, problems then arise when it comes to devising and planning for future investment whilst also supporting non-resource-based sectors. Without question, economic expansion and variation is necessary if there is to be any longevity in Brunei's economic wealth when considering the finite nature of both resources. This is a huge challenge, as acknowledged by the government. Accordingly, in 2007, a framework was devised in mind of achieving development across a thirty-year period, which is seen to encompass the 'Wawasan Brunei 2035', the Outline of Strategies and

Policies for Development (OSPD) and the National Development Plan (NDP). The first one is recognised as a national vision focused on enabling the country to attain a sound and high-value standing in relation to its provision of education and wealth of skilled professionals, as determined through its adherence to internationally recognised standards, providing quality of life whilst also ensuring the presence of an economy that is both dynamic and sustainable, with pleasing levels of income per capita (Singh et al., 2017). At this point in time, however, the ability to evaluate the whole effect of such a plain is not possible; however, too much importance and significance being afforded to minerals has, without question, meant consistent structural barriers have faced the prospect of diversification (Cooke, 2012). In this vein, the more comprehensive and wide-ranging plan has, at its very best, led to restricted development, with the key economic activities implemented by Brunei continuing to be centred on oil and gas.

Brunei is, in essence, recognised as being a somewhat regulated context in consideration to the minimum wage rates, the ease with which people may be 'hired and fired', and the regulations pertaining to working time (Singh et al., 2017). In consideration to Bruneian Labour Law in particular, restrictions surrounding the use of temporary staff for long-term tasks are lacking, with a clearly outlined maximum period for holding a temporary role similarly not outlined (World Bank, 2014). When it comes to redeployment or retraining criteria or indeed severance pay in relation to redundancies, there are none in place, with only a notice period applicable, which differs in line with length of service; furthermore, overtime rates of pay and minimum wage ranges are not implemented, with the only provision afforded to staff the one day of rest each week (ibid.).

Despite the fact that the Trade Union Act of 1961 provides registered trade unions with the ability to operate, whilst also affording workers with a right to freedom of association with unions, it remains that, when it comes to collective bargaining, there is a lack of stipulations and/or provisions, whereas unions are entirely restricted from having any involvement with Global Union Federations (ITUC, 2009). Importantly, there is a dearth of union activity, with the right to strike completely neglected. Furthermore, there is the presence of only three trade unions, which are positioned within the oil and gas industry, and which are likely to be compliant (ExpatFocus, 2015). However, when it comes to the majority of the limited rights afforded by the Bruneian Labour Law, employees falling into the expatriate and migrant labourers groups – which notably make up 40% of all workers – are excluded (ITUC, 2009; ExpatFocus, 2015). Moreover, the execution of any laws pertaining to health and safety are slack and permissive and, irrespective of any attempts made in this regard, the national training framework suffers from a lack of consistent, wide-ranging coverage, with a number of Bruneians seen to suffer from a shortfall of skills for any role requiring skill, with basic roles tending to be avoided by workers (ExpatFocus, 2015).

Although there is a significant degree of ease and flexibility when it comes to hiring and letting staff go, which at first could be considered desirable when it comes to enabling organisations to exploit shareholder value (World Bank, 2014), this still means that employee-employer links are weak (Whitley, 1999). Organisations are better positioned to replace their employees with those actively seeking work who are seen to possess resources, with this done through the external labour market, with organisations also able to recruit or dismiss employees in line with service demand and associated changes (Singh et al., 2017). Otherwise stated, businesses are able to make use of short-term staff and thereby solve HR problems in a short-term way. Nonetheless, it is not likely that employers will consider the shared cognitive potential of their staff as a whole, with a lesser inclination to invest in people; subsequently, staff are not as motivated to develop their own skillset for their employing firm (Whitley, 1999; Aoki, 2010).

Once again, employee delegation will be low at formal levels (Whitley, 1999). When it comes to the law, collective bargaining is not an obligation; accordingly, staff input is then incorporated into employee contracts, with only a very restricted responsibility to consult; staff are not provided with any degree of input when it comes to business organisation issues (Singh et al., 2017). With this noted, it may be stated that, under both practice and law, union countervailing power is lacking; employers are then not required to assign any degree of decision-making to their staff (Whitley, 1999). Despite the fact that delegation is recognised as potentially able to strengthen and highlight mutually beneficial high value-added productive frameworks, when there is a lack of significant relationships with legal incentives and stakeholders, the view may be posited that organisations will then be more likely to opt for short-term value maximisation (Whitley, 1999; Hall & Soskice, 2001).

In regard to indigenisation, pressures may mean there is a significant degree of competition across organisations in what are recognised as more profitable areas of the economy – including oil and gas, more so than any other – with only a small number of educated and highly skilled local staff available, meaning locals will be provided with only low-level staff (see Mellahi & Wood, 2002). Accordingly, one key consideration recognised in this chapter is centred on investigating and examining the degree of internal diversity across the context of Brunei.

Interdependencies among Human Resource Management Practices

Despite there being a number of widely recognised and agreed upon advantages and obstacles within the national institutional context, which will unquestionably affect the extent to which employers delegate to staff (Whitley, 1999), in this chapter, Whitley's definition of interdependence is utilised in such a way so as to incorporate the relative tendency of an organisation to actively invest in its staff and longevity (Whitley, 1999); however, there is acknowledgement regarding the fact that the concept could include a larger number of issues, such as those relating to aims and objectives, and interests (Singh et al., 2017). Importantly, delegation, from the perspective of Whitley, is recognised as the degree to which staff are provided with the ability and opportunity to communicate their views in regard to organisational operation, which could range from individual and direct consultation through to a more representative and collective voice, as noted in various works (Whitley, 1999; Brewster et al., 2007). In the case of better progressed and developed markets, both of these are seen to be significant, whilst lower levels are identified in liberal markets (Whitley, 1999).

In this chapter, the main emphasis is placed on interdependence; this is rationalised in line with the perceived vulnerability of the labour movement in Brunei, as well as the overriding and very apparent disregard of certain considerations of voice in the Bruneian Labour Law (Singh et al., 2017). Importantly, the rights of employees under the law (which are notably recognised as lacking and restricted) will be reflected by turnover, as well as the extent to which recruitment and selection, and career-planning, are afforded adequate levels of care; much more focus needs to be directed towards career-planning if the organisation wants to appear to view staff through the lens of not being merely an easily disposed of commodity (Guest, 2007).

Recruitment and Selection

The view that improved recruitment improves organisational performance is a commonly held perspective (Huselid, 1995; Paauwe, 2009), regardless of the presence of significant discussion surrounding the most appropriate and efficient selection practices to be implemented, in addition to which selection approaches are considered to be most optimal (Guest, 2007); as such, consideration is directed towards the degree of seriousness afforded to selection by firms, and whether or not a wide-ranging selection criteria is implemented by organisations rather than directing their efforts towards only a select few basic issues, including willingness to work for a particular paygrade or a minimal skillset, for example (Singh et al., 2017). This includes various factors, including the previous training, the relative importance assigned to qualifications (both formal and informal), together with an assessment of personal characteristics, such as motivation and work dedication (see, for example, Casson et al., 1998; Mohamed et al., 2013; Darwish et al., 2016).

Training

Studies available in the field state that training has the ability to improve organisational performance and competitiveness whilst at once decreasing the rate of employee turnover (Kalleberg & Moody, 1994; Pfeffer, 1998; Way, 2002; Moideenkutty et al., 2011; Razouk, 2011; Darwish et al., 2013). When it comes to investigating the comparative dedication of the firm in line with the development of employee skillsets, training capabilities needs to be taken into account, alongside the comparative adoption of both informal and formal training (Singh et al., 2017).

Internal Career Opportunities

In a comparable vein, there is much support for the view that organisations that utilise internal promotions to a significant degree achieve improved levels of staff motivation and performance, as well as a lower smaller of turnover (Delery & Doty, 1996; Guest, 1997; Guthrie, 2001; Noe et al., 2006; Joseph & Dai, 2009). Accordingly, in this chapter, we direct our effort towards investigating the degree to which the organisation has outlined promotion strategies and procedures rather than ad-hoc, random decisions.

Institutional Complementarity and HR Practices

One fundamental line of thought in the literature centres on comparative capitalism, which implies that, at any point in time, there are only a small number of practical institutional configurations with the ability to create complete complementarities; in other words, practices and rules across the organisation that work better in achieving the best outcomes for organisations and across the economy overall to an extent greater than what would be achieved through individual interventions (Hall & Soskice, 2001; Hancke et al., 2007; Witcher & Chau, 2014). As such, the majority of the early literature available in this field has placed emphasis on developed economics; in particular, on LMEs (Liberal Market Economies) and CMEs (Coordinated Market Economies).

Does the absence of worker rights vis-à-vis shareholders place Brunei as like a full-fledged Liberal Market Economy, particularly as its GDP per capita is on par with several advanced markets? There are two potential rationalisations as to why this is not true. The first of these focuses on generalised development indices. The UNDP human development index ranking implemented in Brunei is 30, which is viewed as being a good figure; nonetheless, predominantly, this is owing to a significant GNP per capital as a result of oil and gas; when other measures are taken into account, performance is poor, as in the case of mean years' schooling (8.7); a significant portion of the workforce is seen to be lacking when it comes to basic skills (UNDP, 2015). As has been recognised by Bryane (2014), Brunei is recognised as both wealthy and as struggling, and beyond the lucrative oil and gas sector, the country is recognised as being closer to a number of other developing countries than that of the developed world.

Once again, accountability and political voice indices, as well as political rights' egalitarian distribution, position the region far away from more advanced and better progressed LMEs (Chongvilavan, 2014). Although there is a significant wealth of literature concerned with the link between development and democracy, which notably presents the suggestion that there is not always a clear link between the two (Przeworski, 2000), it remains that accountability and political voice present far greater limitations in relation to the corporate and political elite; importantly, a lack of democracy further suggests that there is a need for unions to operate in a narrower political domain, which accordingly means campaigning in relation to different considerations is not always possible unless they are in direct relation to the employee contract (Singh et al., 2017). The second considers the lack of consistency across the skills base, with labour regulations only enforced to a minor degree. Despite the fact that a significant proportion of LME labour force is more likely to be unskilled and occupationally insecure occupationally insecure (Standing, 2011), this is nonetheless counterbalanced when considering the significant volume of labourers with more generalised, common tertiary skillsets, who are recognised as fundamental to those organisations in the high-technology arena (Thelen, 2001). Accordingly, it may be seen that, in emerging markets such as in the case of Brunei, subjective and more random regulations enforcement means different employment relation strategies to those positioned to satisfy fixed rules. From a more generalised perspective, it may be inferred that, as a result, complementarities are not as probable; the latter depend on predictable, well-defined game rules, as well as an infrastructure that is encouraging specific abilities and related employment relationships (even when these may be focused on formalised contracting) (Singh et al., 2017).

The question may then be posed as to whether or not this could possibly position Brunei as somewhat less regulated when compared with other developed LMEs. In this regard, the literature available, as completed in relation to cross-cultural management and native management practices, provides the implication that developing markets are recognised as being more communitarian when compared alongside better developed liberal markets, as highlighted in a number of other works (Morris et al., 1994; Mangaliso, 2001; Tsui, 2004); otherwise stated, social relationships and linked perspectives of obligation and mutuality are far more complex. Subsequently, those organisations achieving success in these particular contexts consider such relationships, aligning the business with such prevailing societal realities and norms (Tsui, 2004; Herrmann & Werbel, 2007). In other words, it may be recognised that informal regulatory mechanisms receive more attention and importance.

Literature developments in the arena of comparative capitalism have been concerned with enhancing this examination through to peripheral European, as well as the developing world as a whole, resulting in the further expansion of a number of different national institutional archetypes, including Familial Capitalism (East Asia), Hierarchical Market Economies (Latin America), Mixed-Market Economies (the Mediterranean world), Segmented Business Systems (tropical Africa), and South East Asian Capitalism (Tipton, 2009; Carney et al., 2009; Steier, 2009; Wood et al., 2011; Hancke et al., 2007; Schneider, 2009). Nonetheless, a shared aspect of these systems is the consistent development and greater degree of institutional support, symmetry across SME and lightly regulated sectors, in one sense, and across more large-scale, more rigidly regulated firms, in another, a specific high-incidence rate across family-based ownership, in combination with an inclination for autocratic-paternalist management (Carney et al., 2009; Wood et al., 2011). Otherwise stated, across these environments, the variations identifiable between smaller organisations and those of a larger size are better positioned to be emphasised (Singh et al., 2017).

In some regard, irrespective of the flaws or shortcomings of the Law in terms of owner rights (La Porta et al., 2000), a dominance of family ownership is nonetheless recognised as able to decrease agency issues and accordingly facilitate the opportunity to manoeuvre when it comes to presenting more innovative practices; on the other hand, however, a lesser number of systematic pressures, including legislation encouraging co-determination and consultation, developed training abilities, or countervailing employee power with the objective to motivate the adoption of the type of cooperative HR practices more commonly experienced in mature coordinated markets (Hall & Soskice, 2001).

The literature available in relation to segmented business systems is comparable in the sense that it highlights the pivotal underpinning part played by informal understandings and rules in certain contexts, as highlighted in the works of Wood and Frynas (2006) and Wood et al. (2011). In essence, this could encompass the significant adoption of more informal networks (such as those of present staff) in the recruitment arena, in addition to a more far-reaching extent of flexibility in regard to leave and rewards (ibid.). Where there is variation in terms of institutional methods in comparison with cross-cultural methods, the former are seen to highlight that particular arrangements are somewhat delicate and potentially unstable, and are seen to co-exist alongside significant inequalities in terms of both resources and power; this can mean production paradigms of greater value are problematic to achieve (ibid.). Moreover, as has been discussed earlier, in the case of emerging markets, Labour Law enforcement is commonly seen to lack consistency, enabling arbitrary managerial power to be present (ibid.). Furthermore, the country is seen to be far-removed from the business systems implemented elsewhere, such as in the context of tropical Africa, for example, with other emerging market capitalist archetypes also demonstrating much difference; importantly, in the similar pursuit of growth and development, oil and gas have achieved reliability, even though such growth is somewhat unpredictable and precarious (Singh et al., 2017). In this regard, reference is made to development and growth patterns in the work of Mellahi and Wood (2002), with specific consideration to petro-states with an abundance of small-to-medium populations, referring to these as *petroleum growth regimes*; in this case, the view may be posited that Brunei adheres to this particular framework. Nonetheless, it may also be suggested that oil and gas revenues and the volatility of such, in addition to the degree to which revenue may be achieved, irrespective of any governance inadequacies, prevents the introduction of a well-aligned combination of institutions that could represent a consistent and logical development process (Jessop, 2012). In this same vein, as has been pinpointed by Boschini et al. (2007), the issues linked to institution-building in petro-states are especially distinct, which accordingly poses problems in providing the required support to achieve the most ideal organisational practices and, as a result, wide-ranging and sustainable development.

One of the key themes identifiable in the studies available on comparative capitalism concerns the overall denial of the concept that HR practices at the organisational level are extensively implemented free from institutional situations (Hancke et al., 2007; Whitley, 1999). It may be posited that, should wide-ranging equally supportive complementarities be restricted to more developed societies, this subsequently would present the view that, across developing markets, different practices and rules identified together would be not as efficiently positioned to achieve greater outcomes in relation to a simple sum of their individual aspects (Hall & Soskice, 2001). As has been highlighted previously, the studies carried out in regard to comparative capitalism imply that, across more developed societies, established institutional models mean that reciprocally supportive informal and formal practices and regulations may be corresponding; in other words, achieving more improved results when compared with the sum of results garnered through separate practices (Hall & Soskice, 2001; Hancke et al., 2007). In consideration to developing markets, those institutions that are less developed and therefore weaker mean that there could be a complete lack of or weaker presence of complementarities (Hancke et al., 2007); subsequently, this implies that there could be only minimal encouragement to adopt a specific national approach to the management of people; otherwise stated, although development and reward initiatives could improve performance, any specific mix of such would not be well positioned to achieve greater outcomes across national economies, predominantly as a result of the complete lack of complementarities (Singh et al., 2017).

HR systems or HR practices that are presented together in a mutually supportive way do not present complementarity in their own right; rather, practices that are combined and that work in unison might not achieve improved outcomes than the sum of their individual aspects in the lack of a supportive institutional setting (Darwish et al., 2016; Singh et al.,

2017). Nonetheless, an extensively implemented HR framework comprising wide-ranging cohesions in practice and policy could be seen to support and correspond to particular aspects of the system, and in combination could present an example of complementarity: as an example, a much greater degree of vocational training and employment security could facilitate organisation-centred and incremental skills development, in addition to various kinds of career planning, where the last of these might deem the former systemic aspects to be more pertinent (Thelen, 2001). On the other hand, when there is an absence of rational, mutually supportive HR systems, there is then a greater chance that institutional shortfalls will be reflected; in this same vein, an abundance of them in particular economic regions would then highlight more vulnerable and less proficient institutional coupling, meaning there would be a far more pronounced presence of internal diversity (Wood and Lane 2012; Goergen et al., 2012).

In this particular case, organisations would not benefit from having as many motivational drivers in regard to designing and implementing a comprehensive and intelligible HR system when compared with more mature contexts; this is owing to the fact that the most important dimensions would be undermined by systematic deficits: as an example, had there been a lack of chronic skills across a particular economy, poaching might have been implemented in order to achieve people investment (Singh et al., 2017). This may be taken to infer that those organisations completing testing across high value-added HR practices are better positioned to ensure care and caution when it comes to individual interventions than methodically associated groups of such, and, when this is done, it is then more unlikely that the most ideal results will be achieved (Singh et al., 2017).

As such, the following proposition has been devised:

Proposition 1: *Systems of greater value-added HR practices are not as well positioned to make more optimal contributions in line with business-related performance when compared with the total of their individual aspects.*

Internal Diversity at the Institutional Level and HR Practices: Are Particular HR Practices Considered More Practical in Consideration to the Sector?

This chapter presents a case study carried out at an individual country level, meaning the impacts stemming from organisations in Brunei, as a whole, cannot be tested besides in relation to complementarities; therefore, there is also a need to assess the degree to which HR practices are more liable to differ in line with the characteristics of the firms (Singh et al., 2017). Nonetheless, as has been emphasised through capitalist diversity studies, organisations are more keenly positioned to have varying impacts in terms of the various types of business across just an individual national context (Wood & Lane, 2012). In this vein, it is maintained that institutional arrangements that are less directly aligned or otherwise more changeable are better positioned to achieve a greater degree of internal diversity across national environments (Wood & Lane, 2012). Accordingly, although diversity across organisational practices is consistently limited by national contextual circumstances, when there is a lack of structure across institutions, or otherwise they are merely in the development stage, there would then be greater pressure on actors to establish and shape their own solutions in line with their more pressing requirements (Jessop, 2012). In this vein, any voids at the national level, notably in regard to informal or formal regulations, could be filled through interventions devised in relation to regional or sector-specific authorities and their associates, and/or more specifically concentrated national legislation so as to satisfy specific requirements, to communicate a more superior inevitability when it comes to exchanging relations in strategic arenas (Jessop, 2012; Wood & Lane, 2012). Otherwise stated, even in the case that institutional arrangements are the focus of the same worldwide patterns or that they share similar aspects, it remains that they would differ within and across different environments and contexts (Jessop, 2012); fluidity or institutional weakness at the national level would be counterbalanced through institutional solutions being implemented in such a way so as to support and encourage particular practices at the organisational level, focused on overcoming common issues across specific industries or arenas (Singh et al., 2017).

Accordingly, a number of the different regulatory groups could be geared towards particular sectors, which might highlight a bottom-up approach to institution-building, with businesses and other stakeholders in a particular sector acting in such a way so as to push formal regulatory solutions and policy in line with their requirements, and/or providing support for and accordingly acting in a way so as to enable mutually acceptable informal regulations to be supported (Boyer, 2006; Jessop, 2012). It could also represent a top-down method, with national governments directing a more dominant degree of focus towards a specific sector for political or ideological reasons, or otherwise owing to the fact it could be identified as being in the government's best interests to do so (Collinge, 2001; Hudson, 2006).

Accordingly, in petro-states, one of the key points of emphasis surrounding institution-building is placed on providing the oil and gas industry with support, as recognised by various academics in the field (Auty, 2002; Mellahi & Wood, 2002), which leads to the view that there is a great deal of diversity in the efficacy and incidence of particular HR practices. Across a number of petro-states, organisations functioning in the gas and oil industry are seen to be very powerful and at the core of government focus (Weinthal & Luong, 2006). Accordingly, it has been noted that, across petro-states, entrepreneurs will fail to consider productive fields of economy activity – specifically that of manufacturing – in an effort to compete for rents (Auty, 1999; Mehlum et al., 2006). Once again, the point may be laboured that skilled labour and capital are steered away from the manufacturing arena in petro-states (ibid.). Lastly, institutions have a tendency to be directed towards providing the oil and gas industry with regulation and support, with a lack of consistency and/or support in regulations, which could encourage a greater degree of HR practices in a number of other economic fields, including services and manufacturing (Singh et al., 2017).

It is emphasised by the Resource Curse that manufacturing may be 'crowded out' predominantly as a result of skills and investments being directed towards the gas and oil sector, with the impacts of over-valuation of currency in a number of other economic areas being experienced, which therefore results in manufacturing, in particular, suffering as a result (Atkinson & Hamilton, 2003; Frankel, 2010; Darwish et al., 2017). In this regard, the one-sided emphasis of institutions and such wide-ranging impacts mean the opportunities of capabilities and technology running into manufacturing are decreased (Papyrakis & Gerlagh, 2004). Lastly, those countries that have a wealth of resources are recognisable by their inadequately balanced development of human capital, which means developing organisation-focused skills in manufacturing and the obstacles of such are more problematic (Van der Ploeg & Poelhekke, 2009). From a practical perspective, there is the insinuation that high value-added HR approaches in manufacturing would be alleviated by high staff turnover rates, undercapitalisation, volatility, and weak institutional support; the oil and gas industry, on the other hand, would witness the opposite (Sachs & Warner, 2001; Weinthal & Luong, 2006). Accordingly, the second proposition below has been devised:

Proposition 2: *The resources and focus directed towards recruitment and selection, training, and to expanding internal career opportunities, and their effects on staff performance and turnover rate, would be relatively low across the manufacturing industry, whilst the oil and gas industry would witness relatively high degrees.*

Internal Diversity at the Institutional Level and HR Practices: Is Size of Relevance in Some Contexts?

As discussed in the work of Bonaccorsi (1992), the size of an organisation is representative of an estimation of business resources. Accordingly, there are a number of clear links to be identified when considering organisational size, and the degree and nature of complex, high-level HR practices (De Kock et al., 2006). Accordingly, in line with the evidence garnered in the Australian context, it has been determined by Kotey and Sheridan (2004) that organisations of a larger size are seen to be more expected to implement formal HR systems, whilst smaller organisations tend to focus on ad-hoc, less formal interventions. When examining the case of North Cyprus, it was determined by Tanova (2003) that smaller organisations were seen to have a greater tendency to adopt informal recruitment approaches; it was further supported through the completion of Canadian studies that larger organisations show a preference for more sophisticated and formalised recruitment strategies (Golhar & Deshpande, 1997).

Despite the fact that bigger organisations are expected to have a wealth of resources that can be directed towards HRM, it remains that there is still a point to be argued in terms of whether, in Brunei, as an example, high value-added HR approaches would be better able to provide performance with more positive contributions (Singh et al., 2017). The comparative literature available in regard to institutional configurations in emerging markets imply that the key area of institutional coverage and the core of both informal and formal regulation would predominantly be centred on businesses of a greater size (Schneider, 2009; Wood et al., 2011). On the other hand, smaller organisations could avoid regulatory arrangements or otherwise only selectively engage with them. Lastly, bigger organisations have a greater tendency to utilise their political power, and are further positioned to secure regulatory interventions that are aligned with their requirements (Singh et al., 2017).

As such, despite the fact that organisation size is all too commonly considered in the HR literature as being a distinct and entirely distinct contextual variable in line with national context, as noted by (Bowen & Ostroff, 2004), it remains that, in the field of comparative institutional analysis, a portion of the literature across emerging economies draws an association between context and organisational size (Singh et al., 2017). In particular, business systems theory extensions to emerging markets imply that these systems may be recognised by specifically distinct separation between bigger organisations, which are comparatively well-regulated, and large and inconsistently regulated small organisations and informal sectors (Wood & Frynas 2006; Wood et al., 2012). Although the first of these is more likely to show alignment with a number of different formal employment relations regulations, the latter, on the other hand, have a greater likelihood to, in the main, disregard structures of formal regulations, showing a preference for working in line with a number of different informal conventions and norms (Singh et al., 2017). In the case of organisations of a lesser size, owing to the fact that staff tend to be easier to replace – and in line with the view of competitiveness being weaker and more reliant on inexpensive resources rather than offering skills (Wood et al., 2011) – it is recognised that, when it comes to organisations investing in promoting organisation-centred human capital, there is not as much incentive. Once again, it is expected that smaller organisations will suffer more negative outcomes stemming from systemic skills shortfalls owing to their inability to lack of desire to recruit employees with a greater skillset, meaning the production framework providing the foundation of their competitiveness will not be improved through this (Singh et al., 2017). Although smaller organisations and the informal sector are recognised by their arbitrary and autocratic managerial power, which is lessened as a result of paternalism, with overly inadequate wages counterbalanced as a result of informal credit, ad hoc compassionate leave, long working hours, and informal recruitment through the adoption of networks comprising existing employees (Wood et al., 2011). This is not to infer, however, that such organisations will unavoidably seek or work to encourage higher value-added HR practices, but rather that efforts would be directed towards achieving regulatory change in mind of facilitating the most desirable types of HR solution (Crouch et al., 2009). Across such developing markets, institutional redesign is possible as a result of the weaknesses identifiable at the institutional level (Ebner et al., 2008). Of course, this means that there is a greater degree of vulnerability identified in the case of the government, with larger organisations able to exercise their power in relation to their corporate interests (Grzymala-Busse, 2008). Otherwise stated, although there are key distinctions to be recognised when comparing smaller firms with larger ones across all contexts, as well as in relation to their comparative positioning to invest in high value-added HR practices, it remains that such distinctions would be especially identifiable in developing market settings (Singh et al., 2017). Accordingly, the third proposition is devised:

Proposition 3: *The comparative emphasis and resources directed towards recruitment, selection and training, in addition to the development of internal career opportunities, and their effects on the performance and turnover rates of staff, will demonstrate growth in relation to the size of the organisation. Otherwise stated, smaller organisations operating in the Brunei context will have lesser regulated and developed HR practices; subsequently, this will mean a greater degree of turnover rate and lesser financial performance. In the case of larger organisations, on the other hand, the impact stemming from such HR practices on performance would be more significant.*

Data

In this particular work, the data utilised has been garnered form a primary survey completed utilising a cross section of organisations. The process implemented in the gathering of data comprised a number of different obstacles. Initially, there was no list available detailing registered organisations operating in the country, meaning there was a need to configure a sample spanning a number of months, making use of various different sources, including the Brunei Economic Development Board, the Brunei government, especially the Ministry of Finance, the Ministry of Industry and Primary Resources, the Chamber of Commerce, in addition to a large number of past government reports (Singh et al., 2017). This approach took a great deal of time owing to the fact that it was common for data not to be up-to-date and also required cross-checking – again, a time-consuming task. Ultimately, however, a sampling framework was created, notably encompassing 465 organisations, with 241 of these utilised for the purpose of a primary survey. The total rate of completion was 151 surveys from a sample of 214, which was recognised as representative of a high rate, notably that of 70%. The main respondents of this work were HR Directors. It is again reiterated that those individuals holding managerial positions are pivotal in communicating a consistent and clear message in regard to the type of HR practices and policies in implementation; this is recognised as able to affect staff responses and performance at the business level (see Bowen & Ostroff, 2004; Wright & Nishi, 2013; Singh et al., 2016, 2017). Accordingly, the views of HR directors in regard to HR practices are fundamental when it comes to garnering insight into the link between performance results and formal practices (for more details in relation to measurement, data, and analysis, see Singh et al., 2017).

Discussion and Conclusions

The work presented in this chapter is focused on examining the link between HRM and performance in consideration to differences across various arenas, including sector, organisational size, and the potential complementarities advantageous to organisations functioning across all Brunei sectors. In other words, examination centres on whether or not HR practices devised in order to encourage a higher degree of interdependence between the employer and employee are not only more commonplace but also seen to be more efficient in terms of achieving more notably organisational performance across bigger organisations and various sectors. It was established that positive perceived financial performance is identifiable when there is the presence of robust recruitment and selection processes, and positive internal career and training prospects, with the first of these practices also seen to contribute to lower employee turnover rates; nonetheless, it was not possible to determine that sets of mutually supportive practices, as facilitated via complementarity, achieve positive outcomes in relation to perceived financial performance (Singh et al., 2017). This work has emphasised that, in contrast to the manufacturing arena, the oil and gas sectors have achieved benefit through their lesser turnover rates when they are incorporated within a well-considered and stringent HR practices – more specifically, training, and recruitment and selection, which are found to provide a strong contribution to achieving decreases in turnover rate. Once again, when it comes to perceived financial performance, when comparing the manufacturing sector with the oil and gas sector, no sectorial differences could be identified, even when the same set of HR practices have been incorporated within the framework (Singh et al., 2017). This is a valuable discovery when taking into account that it may be expected that, across petro-states, a greater degree of attention would be directed towards creating and developing institutions beneficial to the oil and gas industry than manufacturing, facilitating efficient high value-added HR practices in the case of the former (Darwish et al., 2017). Nonetheless, there is also the potential for the interests of the oil and gas sector to be more efficiently served as a result of the keen management in areas of interest than greater regulation: as an example, the potential to fully utilise semi- and unskilled low-wage labour from foreign areas and an overall lack in labour and other law enforcement, meaning that may be preferable to urge and promote an atmosphere of non-threatening regulatory neglect, as highlighted by Sawyer and Gomez (2012). It may also highlight the degree to which the HR requirements across the industry might be easily overcome via directing attention to labour markets in other countries, both for unskilled and skilled labour, with high wage levels facilitating the prepared sourcing of skills in the former instance (Akpomuvie, 2011) and the almost complete lack of legal rights providing discipline-related security in the latter (Abella, 1995). In some regard, the application of high wages for skilled staff and lacking migration status for unskilled staff could ultimately provide some degree of rationalisation for the lower turnover rates witnessed across the sector, the ineffectiveness of combined HR systems notwithstanding (Singh et al., 2017).

Nonetheless, it is pertinent to highlight that the services sector showed a greater degree of financial performance when more emphasis was placed on training, recruitment and selection, and internal career opportunities, all of which may be established as fundamental across the framework, notably affecting perceived financial performance; when compared with other sectors in Brunei, it can be seen that the services sector is keenly segmented between, in one regard, medium and large organisations, with a great degree of formal links to other organisations and a significant alignment with the formal national institutional regime, and then in another regard, small-scale, informal organisations (Singh et al., 2017). Owing to the fact that smaller organisations and the informal sector were not included in this research, the latter reality is seen to be highlighted in the findings. On the other hand, it is then probable that, although variation is expected across the findings, such as in regard to suppliers and principles, as an example, it remains that, in the manufacturing, and oil and gas sectors, the separation is not expected to be as significant when considering the stronger, more complex links between those involved, and also owing to there being a more significant amount of organisations possessing a middle ground in regard to HR practice (see Abdul-Aziz & Zoo Lee, 2007; Golhar & Deshpande, 1997). The findings further emphasise that, irrespective of the occurrence of more complex HR practices, it remains that, with the development of organisations, a more significant employee turnover rate is witnessed, meaning organisations are then more keenly positioned to direct resources towards people investment; notably, this could position them as more susceptible to poaching (Singh et al., 2017). Nonetheless, it was also established that large organisations show a much greater recognised financial performance, which highlights that size is not always responsible for a lack of efficiency or performance; in actuality, it could be that bureaucratic economies of scale may be gained (Brewster et al., 2006). Those organisations that have been in operation for a longer period could also show much lower turnover rates, which could be owing to operational players being recognised as delivering a greater degree of security in their career paths, meaning seeking out other prospects is less appealing (Singh et al., 2017).

When examining the effects of the individual HR practices involved in the propositions detailed in this chapter, it may appear that recruitment and selection practices quality is proficient in identifying those who are more liable to seek out another employer in the future. Importantly, internal career opportunities, training, and recruitment and selection have all been highlighted as significant when it comes to ensuring a positive effect on perceived financial performance, with such impacts further enhanced with greater organisational size (Singh et al., 2017). These results are seen to be in support of a number of other works carried out in this arena (see, for example, Arthur, 1994; Huselid, 1995; Guthrie, 2001; Guthrie et al., 2009; Darwish et al., 2016). Nonetheless, this means there remains the question as to whether or not mutually supportive practices linked with complementarities are then expected to be experienced in environments such as that of Brunei.

Despite the fact that there has been much discussion concerning the systematic implementation of associated systems of HR practice that will achieve more optimal findings than the sum of individual ones, as noted by Ichniowski and Shaw (1999), this view was not supported in this work, with this proposition not validated through the test on HR practices and their internal fit; in contrast, the results garnered through this work have established that the individual effects of HR practices influence performance on an individual basis to a greater relative extent than a more wide-ranging set of practices (Singh et al., 2017). Such findings imply that the most promising configuration might not only be influenced by national context but also by the particular aspects of the organisation and the industry itself, particularly should there be vulnerability identified in terms of central institutional supports; otherwise stated, even in the instance that fully fledged complementarities could not be defined, particular HR practices are seen to be more valuable than others, at least in consideration to organisational characteristics (Singh et al., 2017).

Accordingly, the findings presented in this chapter imply that the HR practices implemented in Brunei that create the most proficient OP would not always align with the familiar sets of practice (whether instrumentalist or cooperative), recognised as creating more efficient outcomes for

Western organisations operational in particular well-established markets (see Hall & Soskice, 2001; Storey, 2007). This could also highlight fluid or partial institutional supports, meaning there would be some degree of difficulty when it comes to supporting more complicated relationship networks that position more complex and interlocking HR systems as practical. Otherwise stated, should complementarities be less developed across emerging markets (Hancke et al., 2007), those practices working together are then not as well positioned to achieve more optimal results than the sum of their individual components could imply (Singh et al., 2017). Without question, there has been much discussion to show that, across petroleum growth-centred initiatives, the challenges facing the HR manager are then likely to be much greater and it would then be more problematic to find a combination of mutually supportive HR practice bundles (Mellahi & Wood, 2002). Despite this work examining those firms operating in the private sector, the results seem to provide support for this view.

A clear rationale across the global policy community implies that light labour market regulation will achieve the very best outcomes for organisations; with this way of thinking providing a foundation for the important very dominant World Bank Doing Business Reports (Cooney et al., 2011). Nonetheless, this work further emphasises that lightly regulated employment findings across various outcomes to the liberal market ideal – and, furthermore, those complementarities linked with such – could be problematic to identify, even when labour markets are seen to be flexible; as an example, a greater volume of employees with restricted schooling, predominantly owing to the less wide-scale tertiary level education, were seen to have a shortage of basic skills, thus positioning them as vulnerable labour and therefore driving a greater degree of employer opportunism, whilst also imposing a more significant investment in basic induction training; this allows even fewer resources for more complex sophisticated HRD (Singh et al., 2017). When there is a lesser degree of restriction on the non-systematic practice of managerial power, as a result of the lack of consistent law enforcement and the restrictions across societal-level balances and checks, the negative outcomes pertaining to insecure tenure could be far more significant. In other words, in such cases, more complex and combined HR models encompass both drawbacks and benefits. It could be seen that some of the negative consequences of a system might be overcome through more informal links and networks, with employers choosing to carry out a role that is seen to be more flexible than that which is more commonly experienced in liberal markets; regardless, however, this work implies that improved selection and recruitment, combined with a greater degree of people-centred investment, can achieve a greater benefit for organisations in their own right (Singh et al., 2017).

As has been discussed, the rationale put forward by the Resource Curse Theory implies that institutional restrictions are a specific aspect of petro-states, meaning that, across these environments, it is more difficult to achieve institutional building (Singh et al., 2019). Amongst other things, resource windfalls mean institutional redesign or building incentives are weakened, with revenue inflow consistently arising even when institutions are poor, whilst volatility in gas and oil prices create problems in long-term investment commitments (Auty, 2003). This could go some way to rationalising the clear lack of complementarities in the Brunei context. Nonetheless, it may be suggested that the results have a greater degree of importance in a number of developing markets where there is a recognised fluidity and fragility across institutional arrangements, and may be seen to be more specifically applicable in the case of small-to-medium petro-states (Singh et al., 2017).

References

Abdul-Aziz, A. R., & Zoo Lee, K. (2007). Knowledge management of foreign subsidiaries of international oil and gas contracting companies. *International Journal of Energy Sector Management, 1*, 63–83.

Abella, M. I. (1995). *Asian migrant and contract workers in the Middle East. The Cambridge survey of world migration.* Cambridge: Cambridge University Press.

Akpomuvie, O. (2011). Tragedy of commons: Analysis of oil spillage, gas flaring and sustainable development of the Niger Delta of Nigeria. *Journal of Sustainable Development, 4*, 200.

Aoki, M. (2010). *Corporations in evolving diversity.* Oxford: Oxford University Press.

Arthur, J. B. (1994). Effects of human resource systems on manufacturing performance and turnover. *Academy of Management Journal, 37*, 670–687.

Atkinson, G., & Hamilton, K. (2003). Savings, growth and the resource curse hypothesis. *World Development, 31*, 1793–1807.

Auty, R. M. (2002). *Sustaining development in mineral economies: The resource curse thesis.* London: Routledge.

Bonaccorsi, A. (1992). On the relationship between firm size and export intensity. *Journal of International Business Studies, 23*, 605–635.

Boschini, A. D., Pettersson, J., & Roine, J. (2007). Resource curse or not: A question of appropriability. *Scandinavian Journal of Economics, 109*, 593–617.

Bowen, D., & Ostroff, C. (2004). Understanding HRM-performance linkages: The role of the "strength" of the HR system. *Academy of Management Review, 29*, 203–221.

Boyer, R. (2006). How to institutions cohere and change. In G. Wood & P. James (Eds.), *Institutions and working life* (pp. 13–61). Oxford: Oxford University Press.

Brewster, C., Wood, G., Croucher, R., & Brookes, M. (2007). Collective and individual voice: Convergence in Europe? *The International Journal of Human Resource Management, 18*, 1246–1262.

Bryane, M. (2014). What does Brunei teach us about using human development index rankings as a policy tool? University of Hong Kong Retrieved from http://papers.ssrn.com/sol3/papers.cfm?abstract_id=2395661.

Carney, M., Gedajlovic, E., & Yang, X. (2009). Varieties of Asian capitalism: Toward an institutional theory of Asian enterprise. *Asia Pacific Journal of Management, 26*, 361–380.

Casson, M., Loveridge, R., & Singh, S. (1998). Human resource management in multinational enterprises: Styles, modes, institutions and ideologies. In G. Hooley, R. Loveridge, & D. Wilson (Eds.), *Internationalization: Process, contexts and markets* (pp. 158–170). Basingstoke: Macmillan.

Chongvilaivan, A. (2014). Inequality in South East Asia. In R. Kanbur, R. Rhee, & J. Zhuang (Eds.), *Inequality in the Asia Pacific* (pp. 303–328). Abingdon: Routledge.

Collinge, C. (2001). Self organization of society by scale. In B. Jessop (Ed.), *Regulation theory and the crisis of capitalism, volume 4 – Developments and extensions* (pp. 176–195). London: Edward Elger.

Cooke, K. (2012). *Brunei Darassalam: Diversifying is hard to do*. Cambridge: Global Briefing. Retrieved from http://www.global-briefing.org/2012/07/diversifying-is-hard-to-do/

Cooney, S., Gahan, P., & Mitchell, R. (2011). Legal origins, labour law and the regulation of employment relations. In M. Barry & A. Wilkinson (Eds.), *Research handbook of comparative employment relations* (pp. 75–97). Cheltenham: Edward Elgar.

Crouch, C., Schroder, M., & Voelzkow, H. (2009). Regional and sectoral varieties of capitalism. *Economy and Society, 38*, 654–678.

Darwish, T., Mohamed, A. F., Wood, G., Singh, S., & Fleming, J. (2017). Can HRM alleviate the negative effects of the resource curse on Firms? Evidence from Brunei. *Personnel Review, 46*, 8, 1931–1947.

Darwish, T., Singh, S., & Mohamed, A. F. (2013). The role of strategic HR practices in organisational effectiveness: An empirical investigation in the country of Jordan. *The International Journal of Human Resource Management, 24*, 3343–3362.

Darwish, T., Singh, S., & Wood, G. (2016), The impact of human resource practices on actual and perceived organizational performance in a Middle-Eastern emerging market. *Human Resource Management, 55*, 261–281.

De Kok, J. M., Uhlaner, L. M., & Thurik, A. R. (2006). Professional HRM practices in family owned-managed enterprises*. *Journal of Small Business Management, 44*, 441–460.

Delery, J. E., & Doty, D. H. (1996). Modes of theorizing in strategic human resource management: Tests of universalistic, contingency, and configurations. Performance predictions. *Academy of Management Journal, 39*, 802–835.

Ebner, A. (2008). Institutional evolution and the political economy of governance. In A. Ebner & N. Beck (Eds.), *The institutions of the market: Organizations, social systems, and governance* (pp. 287–308). Oxford: Oxford University Press.

ExpatFocus (2015). Brunei – employment. Retrieved from http://www.expatfocus.com/expatriate-brunei employment.

Frankel, J. A. (2010). *The natural resource curse: A survey (No. w15836)*. Cambridge, MA: National Bureau of Economic Research.

Goergen, M., Brewster, C., Wood, G., & Wilkinson, A. (2012). Varieties of capitalism and investments in human capital. *Industrial Relations, 51*, 501–527.

Golhar, D. Y., & Deshpande, S. P. (1997). HRM practices of large and small Canadian manufacturing firms. *Journal of Small Business Management, 35*, 30–38.

Grzymala-Busse, A. (2008). Beyond clientelism: Incumbent state capture and state formation. *Comparative Political Studies, 41*, 638–673.

Guest, D. E. (1997). Human resource management and performance: A review and research agenda. *The International Journal of Human Resource Management, 8,* 263–276.

Guest, D. E. (2007). Human resource management and the worker: Towards a new psychological contract? In P. Boxall, J. Purcell, & P. Wright (Eds.), *The Oxford handbook of human resource management* (pp. 128–146). Oxford: Oxford University Press.

Guthrie, J. P. (2001). High-involvement work practices, turnover, and productivity: Evidence from New Zealand. *Academy of Management Journal, 44,* 180–190.

Guthrie, J. P., Flood, P., Liu, W., & MacCurtain, S. (2009). High performance work systems in Ireland: Human resource and organizational outcomes. *The International Journal of Human Resource Management, 20,* 112–125.

Hall, P., & Soskice, D. (2001). An Introduction to the varieties of capitalism. In P. Hall & D. Soskice (Eds.), *Varieties of capitalism* (pp. 1–68). Oxford: Oxford University Press.

Hancke, B., Rhodes, M., & Thatcher, M. (2007). Introduction. In B. Hancke, M. Rhodes, & M. Thatcher (Eds.), *Beyond varieties of capitalism* (pp. 3–38). Oxford: Oxford University Press.

Heeks, R. (1998). Small enterprise development and the 'Dutch Disease' in a small economy: The case of Brunei. Retrieved February 1, 2014, from http://ageconsearch.umn.edu/ bitstream/30563/1/dp980056.pdf.

Herrmann, P., & Werbel, J. (2007). Promotability of host-country nationals: A cross-cultural study. *British Journal of Management, 18,* 281–293.

Hudson, R. (2006). The production of institutional complementarity? The case of North East England. In G. Wood & P. James (Eds.), *Institutions and working life* (pp. 104–122). Oxford: Oxford University Press.

Huselid, M. (1995). The impact of human resource management practices on turnover, productivity, and corporate financial performance. *Academy of Management Journal, 38,* 635–672.

Ichniowski, C., & Shaw, K. (1999). The effects of human resource management systems on economic performance: An international comparison of U.S. and Japanese plants. *Management Science, 45,* 704–721.

ITUC-International Trade Union Confederation (2009). *Annual survey of violations of trade union rights – Brunei Darussalam,* Retrieved June 11, 2009 from http://www.refworld.org/docid/4c52cafdc.html.

Jessop, B. (2012). Rethinking the diversity and variability of capitalism: On variegated capitalism in the world market. In C. Lane & G. Wood (Eds.), *Institutions, internal diversity and change* (pp. 209–237). London: Routledge.

Kalleberg, A. L., & Moody, J. W. (1994). Human resource management and organizational performance. *American Behavioral Scientist, 37,* 948–962.

Kotey, B., & Sheridan, A. (2004). Changing HRM practices with firm growth. *Journal of Small Business and Enterprise Development, 11,* 474–485.

La Porta, R., Lopez-de-Silanes, F., Shleifer, A., & Vishny, R. (2000). Investor protection and corporate governance. *Journal of Financial Economics, 58,* 3–27.

Mangaliso, M. P. (2001). Building competitive advantage from ubuntu: Management lessons from South Africa. *Academy of Management Executive, 15,* 23–33.

Mehlum, H., Moene, K., & Torvik, R. (2006). Institutions and the resource curse*. *The Economic Journal, 116*(508), 1–20.

Mellahi, K., & Wood, G. (2002). Desperately seeking stability: The making and remaking of the Saudi Arabian petroleum growth regime. *Competition and Change, 6,* 345–362.

Mohamed, A. F., Singh, S., Irani, Z., & Darwish, T. (2013). An analysis of recruitment, training and retention practices in domestic and multinational enterprises in the country of Brunei Darussalam. *The International Journal of Human Resource Management, 24,* 2054–2081.

Moideenkutty, U., Al-Lamki, A., & Sree Rama Murthy, Y. (2011). HRM practices and organizational performance in Oman. *Personnel Review, 40,* 239–251.

Morris, M. H., Davis, D. L., & Allen, J. W. (1994). Fostering corporate entrepreneurship: Crosscultural comparisons of the importance of individualism versus collectivism. *Journal of International Business Studies, 25,* 65–89.

Nguyen, Q. T. K. (2014). The regional strategies of British multinational subsidiaries in South East Asia. *British Journal of Management, 25,* S60–S76.

Noe, R., Hollenbeck, J., Gerhart, B., & Wright, P. (2006). *Human resources management: Gaining a competitive advantage.* New York, NY: McGraw-Hill.

Paauwe, J. (2009). HRM and performance: Achievements, methodological issues and prospects. *Journal of Management Studies, 46,* 129–142.

Papyrakis, E., & Gerlagh, R. (2004). The resource curse hypothesis and its transmission channels. *Journal of Comparative Economics, 32,* 181–193.

Pfeffer, J. (1998). Seven practices of successful organizations. *California Management Review, 40,* 96–124.

Podsakoff, P. M., & Organ, D. W. (1986). Self-reports in organizational research: Problems and prospects. *Journal of Management, 12,* 531–544.

Przeworski, A. (2000). *Democracy and development.* Cambridge: Cambridge University Press.

Razouk, A. (2011). High-performance work systems and performance of French small- and medium-sized enterprises: Examining causal order. *The International Journal of Human Resource Management, 22,* 311–330.

Rugman, A. M., & Oh, C. H. (2013). Why the home region matters: Location and regional multinationals. *British Journal of Management, 24,* 463–479.

Sachs, J. D., & Warner, A. M. (2001). The curse of natural resources. *European Economic Review, 45,* 827–838.

Sawyer, S., & Gomez, E. T. (2012). *The politics of resource extraction.* Palgrave Macmillan: Multinational Corporations and the State.

Schneider, B. (2009). Hierarchical market economies and varieties of capitalism in Latin America. *Journal of Latin American Studies, 41,* 553–575.

Singh, S., Darwish, T., & Potocnik, K. (2016). Measuring organizational performance: A case for subjective measures. *British Journal of Management, 27,* 214–224.

Singh, S., Darwish, T., Wood, G. & Mohamed. A. F. (2017). Institutions, complementarity, human resource management and performance in a South-East Asian Petrostate: The case of Brunei. *The International Journal of Human Resource Management, 28,* 18, 2538–2569.

Singh, S., Wood, G., Darwish, T., Fleming, J. & Mohammed, A. F. (2019), Human resource management in multinational and domestic enterprises: A comparative institutional analysis in Southeast Asia. *Thunderbird International Business Review, 61,* 229–241.

Standing, G. (2011). *Precariat: The new dangerous class.* London: Bloomsbury.

Steier, L. P. (2009). Familial capitalism in global institutional contexts: Implications for corporate governance and entrepreneurship in East Asia. *Asia Pacific Journal of Management, 26,* 513–535.

Storey, J. (2007). *Human resource management: A critical text.* New York, NY: Routledge.

Tanova, C. (2003). Firm size and recruitment: Staffing practices in small and large organisations in north Cyprus. *Career Development International, 8,* 107–114.

Thelen, K. (2001). Varieties of labour politics in the developed democracies. In P. Hall & D. Soskice (Eds.), *Varieties of capitalism* (pp. 71–103). Oxford: Oxford University Press.

Tipton, F. B. (2009). Southeast Asian capitalism: History, institutions, states, and firms. *Asia Pacific Journal of Management, 26,* 401–434.

Tsui, A. S. (2004). Contributing to global management knowledge: A case for high quality indigenous research. *Asia Pacific Journal of Management, 21,* 491–513.

UNDP. (2015). Human Development Reports. Retrieved from http://hdr.undp.org/en/content/table-1-human-development-index-and-its-components.

Van der Ploeg, F., & Poelhekke, S. (2009). Volatility and the natural resource curse. *Oxford Economic Papers, 61,* 727–760.

Way, S. (2002). High Performance work systems and intermediate indicators of firm performance within the US small business sector. *Journal of Management, 28,* 765–785.

Weinthal, E., & Luong, P. J. (2006). Combating the resource curse: An alternative solution to managing mineral wealth. *Perspectives on Politics, 4,* 35–53.

Whitley, R. (1999). *Divergent capitalisms.* Oxford: Oxford University Press.

Witcher, B. J., & Chau, V. S. (2012). Varieties of capitalism and strategic management: Managing performance in multinationals after the global financial crisis. *British Journal of Management, 23,* S58–S73.

Wood, G., Dibben, P., Stride, C., & Webster, E. (2011). HRM in Mozambique: Homogenization, path dependence or segmented business system? *Journal of World Business, 46,* 31–41.

Wood, G., & Frynas, J. G. (2006). The institutional basis of economic failure: Anatomy of the segmented business system. *Socio-Economic Review, 4,* 239–277.

Wood, G., & Lane, C. (2012). Institutions, change and diversity. In C. Lane & G. Wood (Eds.), *Capitalist diversity and diversity within capitalism* (pp. 1–31). London: Routledge.

World Bank. (2014). Labour market regulation in Brunei. *Doing business – Measuring business regulations.* Washington: World Bank. Retrieved from http://www.doingbusiness.org/data/exploreeconomies/brunei/labor-market-regulation.

6 Resource Cursed Economies and HR Practices

Tamer K Darwish, Pengiran Muda Abdul Fattaah, Geoffrey Wood, and Satwinder Singh

Introduction

In consideration to the literature available on the 'resource curse', organisations functioning in national economies with a recognised wealth of oil and gas are seen to experience notable obstacles in achieving a competitive edge (Darwish et al. 2017). This is predominantly seen to be as a result of the oil and gas sector to cause an overflow of investment across human and physical capital in other domains linked with governance issues, a propensity for policymakers to turn to oil and gas to overcome developmental issues as opposed to encouraging more wide-ranging institution-building, and the over-valuation and associated instability of currency (Collier 2010; Ross 2012). In a number of different petro-states, the oil and gas sector is seen to be well controlled and regulated, whereas there is a complete neglect in this regard when it comes to non-resource sectors (Auty 1993; Singh et al. 2019). In the case of such difficult situations, it may be suggested that the human aspects of business competitiveness are bestowed with specific value. In consideration to the case of the micro-petro-state, namely that of Brunei, this chapter presents empirical work which examines the degree to which HR practices could prove valuable in overcoming negative sectoral impacts, drawing a comparison between the case of organisations functioning in the oil and gas sector with those functioning in other sectors, and further determines the comparative lessons to be made in striving to garner insight into the possible performance-related outcomes of HR interventions in resource-centred national economies.

When it comes to investigating the association between HR practices and performance, the effects of strategic HR implementation and devolvement across businesses have attracted much attention (see, for example, Pfeffer 1998; Budhwar 2000; Paauwe 2009; Guest 2011; Sheehan 2012; Singh et al. 2012b; Darwish et al. 2015). The incorporation of HRM in the design of business strategy is commonly referred to as strategic HR involvement (SHRI); in contrast, HR devolvement (SHRD) may be referred to as the decentralisation of the main HR practices to Line Managers, meaning personnel specialists are not assigned in this regard (Brewster and Larsen 1992; Darwish and Singh 2013). There is the view that HR practices and policies being incorporated within business and corporate strategy could improve general organisational performance (OP), with HR devolution recognised in the same vein, which could mean any obstacles arising as a result of context may be improved upon (see Cunningham and Hyman 1999; Budhwar 2000; Andersen et al. 2007; Karami et al. 2008; Sheehan 2012). Nonetheless, various works carried out in this vein have been completed in a Western context; therefore, this chapter provides an effort to fill this void by directing emphasis to the case of a developing marketing petro-state.

In particular, the effects of specific SHRI and SHRD on staff turnover are investigated, with managerial views pertaining to financial performance across all sectors in Brunei further considered in light of whether such interventions are able to improve upon the obstacles associated with functioning in a non-resource sector in a resource-rich region. Notably, the country is recognised as being generally well developed and as a stable Southeast Asian country with a number of rich nature resources. The view may also be given that organisations functioning in similar markets, in addition to commodity-driven economies, may be well positioned to learn a number of lessons from what Brunei has achieved, particularly in regard to differences and the obstacles experienced in non-oil and gas sectors in these regions.

The Resource Curse and Organisational Competitiveness

Literature available on the resource curse highlights resource-rich regions as most predominantly characterised by a less stable macro-economic performance when contrasted alongside those with a lesser abundance of mineral riches (Auty 1993; Alexeev and Conrad 2009; Anderson and Ross 2010; Bhattacharya and Hodler 2010). This may be owing to the inclination of currencies to be over-valued; meaning that there is a lesser degree of competitiveness in other sectors, with investors instead focusing on achieving easy returns from minerals in addition to ensuring profitable contracts from governments offering royalty enrichments (Darwish et al. 2017). Subsequently, the latter demonstrate fewer incentives when it comes to motivating the improvements in of institutions and linked policies geared towards achieving more wide-ranging economic development or the encouragement and support of (developmental) initiatives that may be viewed as problematic to support without ongoing financial support, meaning across-sector performance may be inconsistent and unstable (Collier 2010; Ross 2012). In this vein, critics have implemented charges across those countries that benefit from natural resource windfalls (Haber and Menaldo 2001; Alexeev and Conrad 2009). Nonetheless, studies carried out more recently highlight the view that such works have taken into account specific countries and time periods; during what is recognised as a period of historically high and volatile commodity prices, the various obstacles experienced in encouraging wide-ranging development from natural resource increases have become more powerful (Andersen and Ross 2015; Wiens et al. 2014). This then causes a number of questions to arise in regard to implications for HRM. Primarily, the specifically inconsistent and unbalanced nature of development is then expected to result in a skills gap across non-resource industries in the economy (Nuur and Laestadius 2010). Secondarily, in the State sector, lucrative protected job opportunities, as well as oil and gas organisations aiming to achieve authorities' goodwill, results in significant degrees of employee turnover, which subsequently induces a drain of talent from other economic areas (Mellahi and Wood 2002; Mellahi 2007). In a comparable vein, when considering that oil and gas donations could potentially increase political stakes (Bhattacharya and Hodler 2010), petro-state governments commonly aim to further develop employment in an effort to encourage stability; subsequently, this could mean that human resources in other economic fields are stripped, which ultimately causes difficulties for employers in the latter to achieve productivity or implement discipline (Darwish et al. 2017). Essentially, as opposed to dealing with efforts to improve productivity or work in other areas, staff may then look at opting out and instead direct their attention towards more substantial welfare provisions or, alternatively, more favourable sheltered employment.

When aiming to deal with these obstacles, the view may be posited that the comparative development of the HR function, enables management to provide flexible responses to these daily obstacles, and entrusting HR with a fundamental strategic value, enabling a more proficient allocation of resources to the development of internal training and skills, and to encourage retention, is fundamental; nonetheless, in this same way, an inadequate volume of resources could mean greater problems in this area, with contextual circumstances potentially too overwhelming to facilitate positive outcomes from HR interventions (Mellahi 2007).

Context

Brunei may be described as a quickly developing micro-petro-state; in much the same way as other regions of a comparable status, Brunei may be recognised by its generally strong presence of foreign multinationals and its significant number of expatriate workers, both in the skilled professionals arena and that of semi-skilled and unskilled (Darwish et al. 2017). It is possible that professional expatriates could come to face a number of problems when it comes to adapting to the local environments and its cultures; however, they offer unique capabilities, insights, and skills (Singh et al. 2019). On the other hand, in the case of those employees recognised as semi-skilled and unskilled, such individuals are more likely to be given only low wages and corresponding low-status work, with dismissal and deportation likely in the event of poor performance (Santoso 2009). In the case of Brunei, net migration rate is recognised as 2.4 migrant(s)/1000 in 2015 (CIA 2016). Moreover, an estimated 200,000 people are identified making up the employee base – both unemployed and employed; it was established that, in regard to the labour force participation rate, this was 68%, with an estimated 55,000 employed by the public sector whereas more than 91,000 are employed by the private sector; in consideration to those who are employed, the percentage making up Brunei citizens is 53.7% whereas 46.3% are recognised as temporary residents (Darwish et al. 2017). Notably, the government of Brunei has stated that, in consideration to the requirement for greater diversity across the economy, a much larger labour force would be required; nonetheless, it is recognised that migrant workers need to enable diversification plans owing to the fact that the key Bruneian local labour force shows a penchant for roles in the public sector as a result of such work providing both stability and security (Tasie 2009). Furthermore, in consideration to local employees, these are seen to achieve advantages through indigenisation legislation; in regional terms, such individuals are positioned to gain access to a valuable skills and training development system on a local vocation basis, predominantly as a result of good job roles being available in the public sector, with locals seen to show a disinclination to adopt skilled and technical roles in the private field (Minnis 2000). Such a significantly segmented labour force means the challenges of the HR manager, particularly in the case of multinationals, are especially problematic; once again, such a situation could imply that HR function development might garner specific advantages; due to the variation in workforce needing to be managed between Line Managers, the organisation might be positioned to benefit from a more in-depth insight in relation to the abilities and requirements of specific groups of employee (Darwish et al. 2017). In a comparable vein, although there are key approaches to management, it is nonetheless expected that improved HRM opportunities in regard to adopting a strategic role could mean the firm is more responsive to each of the group's abilities, requirements, and potential.

In a comparable vein to various other oil-rich countries, the economy of Brunei has come to face a number of peaks and dips as dictated by the worldwide market, with economic growth demonstrating an average 2.8% average growth in the 2000s, with a key dependence on oil and gas production. Brunei's economy, without question, needs to be dependent on the gas and oil industries to a lesser degree, with the gas industry making up more than half (60%) of all GDP, and a large majority of the country's overall exports (OECD 2014). Importantly, Brunei is seen to be the fourth most significant oil producer in the Southeast Asian region, with ASEAN countries, Australia, India, Japan, New Zealand, and

South Korea recognised as the key destinations of export; furthermore, when examining the issue of the exportation of liquefied natural gas, Brunei is seen to be the ninth largest exporter, with most exported to both South Korea and Japan in the form of liquefied natural gas (Darwish et al. 2017). In consideration to the significant dependence shown by this country towards the oil and gas arena, the overall progression of the country's private sector has been influenced; more specifically, a consistent 20% has, during more recent years, been contributed to GDP by the non-oil and gas industries (OECD 2014). Owing to the country's reliance on oil and gas industries, a larger government sector is now apparent in Brunei; this has restricted the private sector's overall opportunities and role (Darwish et al. 2017). The domination of the industries has been reinforced by the low productivity coupled with high labour wages, where the former is recognised as a factor in the lack of international competitiveness demonstrated by the private sector (Lawrey 2010; OECD 2014).

Moreover, as considered above, in the case of those economies that are commodity-focused, it is likely that there will be a significant degree of variation witnessed at a practical level when examining the minerals and non-minerals sector; in regard to the various obstacles being experienced by non-primary commodities-centred industries, the point may be made that competitiveness's human aspect is then expected to be assigned with specific value in the case of the latter (Darwish et al. 2017). Accordingly, emphasis in this chapter is placed on sector, with the differences between the oil and gas, and non-oil and -gas industries, highlighted.

HR Practice and Performance

Strategy, HR Involvement and HR Devolvement

The literature available in regard to HR involvement and devolvement considers the idea as some type of business dedication to the strategic management of people (Truss and Gratton 1994; Darwish and Singh 2013). In the case that people are recognised as being the most highly valued asset of a firm and need to be optimally deployed in an effort to attain business-related objectives, then, in an effort to do so, there is a need for them to be efficiently involved and integrated across an organisation's strategic activities; again, the point may be laboured that the daily issues of HR facing Line Managers could allow the HR department to focus on other considerations pertaining to strategy, as highlighted by various scholars (Cunningham and Hyman 1999; Budhwar 2000; Singh et al. 2012a). More keenly associating HR function with the overall strategic decision-making process of the firm acknowledges the value of efficient and effective HRM in terms of securing a consistent and long-term competitive edge (Budhwar 2000; Truss et al. 1997). As highlighted earlier, HR devolvement centres on HR practices being assigned to the Line Managers, which of course requires that they are entrusted with administering and adopting such tasks as a direct result of their closeness with their subordinates, thus facilitating their control, management, and motivation (Cunningham and Hyman 1999; Budhwar and Khatri 2001). Such tasks being devolved to Line Management assists in overcoming obstacles and problems that otherwise would warrant clear insider insight, which can at times be too complex for top management to deal with independently (Darwish et al. 2017). The point has also been made that more intimate links and interactions between the HR Director and Line Manager can mean the former is able to garner a more in-depth insight into the issues across various organisational functions and to facilitate quicker responses to staff concerns (Sullivan 2003). In addition, it may also allow the HR function to adopt a more effective and operational part in the strategic process of the firm (Darwish and Singh 2013). Furthermore, HR devolvement and HR involvement can together facilitate a more efficient adoption for High Performance Work Systems (HPWSs) across firms; when these are lacking, HPWSs are not considered practical. It is further stated that organisations encompassing efficient HPWSs share and are transparent with information in regard to business-centred goals and strategy, where staff are able to appreciate and acknowledge the valuable connection between business strategy and HR practices (Darwish et al. 2017). As a result, this allows the perceived significance of HPWS whilst also enabling a significant degree of strategic HR integration (see Lawler 1992; Becker and Huselid 1998; Pfeffer 1998; Evans and Davis 2005; Bowen and Ostroff 2004). In contrast, empowerment is further viewed as being a fundamental organisational practice that also enables HPWS in its positive link to business performance (Pfeffer 1998; Huang 2000).

HRM and Organisational Performance (OP)

The literature considering the link between performance and HR interventions is vast, although varied results are detailed in such works (see Rogers and Wright 1998; Paauwe 2009; Guest 1997, 2011; Darwish et al. 2013; Singh et al. 2016, 2017). In consideration to the latter, this chapter primarily aims to present a further assessment of the strength and nature of any and all connections as an initial point for the investigation of contextual variations. Variation within and across the findings could highlight the wide-ranging and all-encompassing discussion as to how organisational performance can be defined, highlighting not only differences from one national accounting standard to the next, but also how strong performance can be signified and for whom (Rogers and Wright 1998). Accordingly, organisations will be encouraged by both formal and informal rules to implement particular groups of HR practice, with the recognition that a number of high value-added HR models will also achieve much more efficient results than others (ibid.; Brewster et al. 2007). Otherwise stated, the choice, sustainability and viability of particular HR models and related work systems are clearly intimately associated with contextual circumstances (Darwish et al. 2017).

It is recognised in the resource curse literature that institutional configurations are more dominantly focused on serving the minerals sector, with investment capital and talent subsequently seen to be drained from other economic domains (Auty 1993; Mellahi 2007; Nuur and Laestadius 2010). The notable backwash effects such as these suggest that strategic HR interventions across organisations in the latter economic domain will not be as effective when it comes to decreasing staff turnover rates and improving organisational performance (Darwish et al. 2017).

Accordingly, the following two propositions are outlined:

1   A negative relationship can be identified between strategic HR involvement and HR devolvement, and employee turnover; where involvement and devolvement are seen to be greater, employee turnover rate will be lower. Nonetheless, such effects are seen to be focused in the oil and gas sector.
2   A positive relationship can be identified between strategic HR involvement and HR devolvement, and perceived financial performance; where involvement and devolvement are seen to be greater, perceived financial performance will be higher. Nonetheless, such effects are seen to be focused in the oil and gas sector.

As can be seen above, as documented in the resource curse literature, in those countries identified as mineral resource-rich, other economic areas strive to compete; thus, organisations such as these are then expected to be forced into a position of basic survival, with a notably lesser volume of resources able to be directed towards strategic HR issues (Darwish et al. 2017). Otherwise stated, should strategic HRM be able to improve upon the various obstacles facing non-resource sector operations, this may not be as probable. The resource curse literature makes the point that those interventions implemented in-firm are not as likely to improve upon the negative effects of operating in a resource-rich arena (Auty 1993). Accordingly, the third proposition is outlined:

3   Significant differences will be identifiable between oil and gas and non-oil and gas sectors when there is a presence of strategic HR involvement and HR devolvement. Non-oil and gas sector direct much less attention towards SHRI and HRD issues when contrasted alongside the oil and gas sector.

To examine the above propositions, data has been garnered form a primary survey completed by HR directors utilising a cross section of organisations in Brunei. The total rate of completion was 151 surveys from a sample of 214, which was recognised as representative of a high rate, notably that of 70% (for more details in relation to measurement, data, and analysis, see Darwish et al. 2017).

Discussion and Conclusions

A number of key differences have been identified across sectors in regard to performance consequences in relation to the arrangement of HR management. It was further established that strategic HR involvement is significantly influential when it comes to decreasing the turnover rate of staff within the non-oil and -gas sector; across the oil and gas sector, such variations were not identified, which could mean that the sector's structural dynamics are reflected, with employment viewed as being far more necessary than other areas (beyond the public sector), although a high rate of the poaching of skilled employees was witnessed in the pursuit of satisfying indigenisation quotas (Darwish et al. 2017). In a number of petro-states, somewhat privileged 'insider' groupings of indigenous nationals were seen to frequently involve themselves in role-hopping and/or even rejecting challenging employment in favour of cosier State positions, whereas the most talented, skilled and productive of employees were seen to strive to secure a role with a more lucrative position in the oil and gas sector unless organisations across other domains were seen to proactively adopt measures focused on retention (Mellahi and Wood 2002; Mellahi 2007; Darwish et al. 2017). At once, this highlights that HR interventions at the organisational level are influential in overcoming a number of the problems inherent in the non-resource sectors. Nonetheless, from an across-economy perspective, HR devolvement was not seen to have an impact, which could potentially highlight the degree to which devolvement might epitomise a variation of realities; accordingly, while the first might be to redirect a significant portion of daily administration over to frontline HR staff, thereby enabling the HR department to direct their attention towards more wide-ranging strategic considerations, the second might highlight an altogether lack of HR function, with foundational HR administration carried out at the frontline but with a lack of more wide-ranging HR abilities (Darwish et al. 2017).

Nonetheless, although one aspect of the majority of petro-states is a significantly segmented labour market identified at the organisational level of HR management, this does not necessarily infer that HR managers' involvement in outlining strategy is without effect; in actual fact, it would seem to have a positive impact on performance from a general perspective (Darwish et al. 2017). Regardless, however, HR devolvement seems to exhibit significantly positive performance consequences for those organisations operating in non-resource sectors; once again, this could highlight the lack of clarity in the concept of HR devolvement; a number of organisations in the non-oil and -gas sector continue to be locked into a basic cost-cutting approach, meaning that, in such circumstances, well developed central managerial administrative functions could be recognised as financially untenable (Darwish et al. 2017).

As a conclusion, much sectoral divergence was witnessed when examining the issue of strategic HR involvement in the case of central issues of business-related strategy, with clearly comparable practices in the vein of devolvement; nonetheless, it is likely that the former will shape and influence the latter, with devolvement seen to either highlight an overall intensity of the HR department on strategic issues, or otherwise an entirely inadequate ability and shortage of resource in the case of the latter (Darwish et al. 2017). Nonetheless, across a number of different petro-states encompassing significant foreign labour forces carrying out both unskilled and semi-skilled positions, HR devolvement can also highlight problematic aspects, regardless of industry. As is widely recognised, foreign workers tend to have very few legal rights, and it may therefore be seen that desire for HR devolvement in such a situation could similarly highlight an inclination to repeal responsibility for the low value-added 'dirty work' of adopting authoritarian approaches to employment and work onto low-level management and frontline staff (Darwish et al. 2017; Singh et al. 2019).

As a result of the above, a number of key concerns are raised in the field of HR practice. Primarily, there is the possibility that HR management, when faced with more difficult situation, will encourage higher value-added and more ethically centred HR practices; this work has highlighted the overall comparative authorisation of HR management as being intimately aligned with sectorial dynamics; as such, it is expected that such 'norm entrepreneurship' would further support existing internal diversity, as opposed to facilitating in filling the void in practice between oil and gas, and other industries (Darwish et al. 2017). Second, the research has emphasised the degree to which long historical legacies – and drawbacks – both within and across national institutional contexts, could pose a number of problems to overcome, with the practicality of both strategic methods of HPWS and HRM reliant on situations (Brewster et al. 2007). This is not to state that organisation-level innovation cannot be achieved or that there is the potential for fresh strategic initiatives; in actual fact, the spectrum of choices and results may be facilitated or restricted by situations (Darwish et al. 2017).

A wealth of foreign investment has been attracted into Brunei during more recent periods, with these predominantly witnessed following oil and gas; however, across a number of petro-states, the non-oil and -gas industries have come to experience a number of critical obstacles when aiming to achieve a competitive edge (Singh et al. 2019). This work has identified the urgency with which HR Directors in Brunei need to adopt a more wide-ranging role spanning beyond HRM and its daily technicalities. Furthermore, embedded local prejudices should be followed in contrast with less skilled categories of 'guest' workers, meaning that involvement in HR issues becomes counter-productive (Santoso 2009). Accordingly, should organisations functioning across the non-oil and -gas sectors in petro-states come to experience the fundamental, inherent issues stemming from competitiveness, it might become apparent that HRM is not only more important but also lacking in resource; in this case, firms might need to function at a lower level of survival, and would then show greater hesitancy in investing in any area outside of those critical to operations (Darwish et al. 2017). These behaviours might also be manifested in other petro-states in consideration to comparable 'resource curse' reasons; of course, support garnered in the context of the Kingdom of Saudi Arabia implies that those organisations operating beyond the oil and gas sector have experienced a number of critical HR challenges in regard to resources, skills, and establishing a sustainable competitive edge (Mellahi and Wood 2002; Budhwar and Mellahi 2006). One valuable path of further research to be explored in the future could be the compilation of research evidence from other areas, where the latter would be able to position and encourage a particular HR practice model in petro-states, and in establishing which aspects of practice are most unique to Brunei; further, a more intimate analysis pertaining to the relative efficacy of HR devolvement and workforce composition in contexts such as that of Brunei could also garner some valuable knowledge into the obstacles linked with the management of various other expatriate groups (Darwish et al. 2017).

This chapter presents an empirical work that is centred on the completion of a single country case study, but nonetheless provides support for other works carried out in the field of HR across petro-states (Mellahi 2007). A productive foundation for further work could involve widening the panel of petro-state country cases; there is recognised potential for petro-states with a greater degree of corporate governance structure and developed institutions to showcase a less pronounced segmentation, meaning a greater position in terms of skills development and more mature training, along with a greater degree of balance across organisations in the national economy (Mehlum et al. 2006; Darwish et al. 2017).

Although literature carried out on the resource curse implies that organisations operating in non-oil and gas industries in petro-states continue to experience obstacles induced at the structural level, it remains that a number of the negative HR consequences may be improved upon through strategic choice; more specifically, in consideration to organisations' management of their staff (Darwish et al. 2017). The empirical work presented in this chapter has provided support for the view that people management is fundamental and highly influential, even in the case of marginalised areas of national economies. Nonetheless, although organisations in the latter arena are not as well positioned to offer the resources or abilities to facilitate strategic HRM function ability, it remains that introducing structural institutional change is far more problematic than improving the role of people management; to this end, this would enable some portion of the solution to be presented in relation to context-based problems (Darwish et al. 2017).

References

Alexeev, M. and Conrad, R. (2009). The elusive curse of oil. *The Review of Economics and Statistics*, 91, 3, 586–598.

Andersen, J. and Ross, M. (2015). The big oil change: a closer look at the Haber-Menaldo analysis. *Comparative Political Studies*, 47, 7, 993–1021.

Andersen, K., Cooper, B. and Zhu, C. (2007). The effect of SHRM practices on perceived firm financial performance: some initial evidence from Australia. *Asia Pacific Journal of Human Resources*, 45, 2, 168–179.

Auty, R. (1993). *Sustaining Development in Mineral Economies: The Resource Curse Thesis*. Routledge, London.

Becker, B.E. and Huselid, M.A. (1998). High performance works systems and firm performance: a synthesis of research and managerial implications. In Rowland, K.M. and Ferris, G.R. (Eds), *Research in Personnel and Human Resource Management*, Vol. 16, JAI, Greenwich, CT, pp. 53–101.

Bhattacharya, S. and Hodler, R. (2010). Natural resources, democracy, and corruption. *European Economic Review*, 54, 4, 608–621.

Bowen, D.E. and Ostroff, C. (2004). Understanding HRM-firm performance linkages: the role of the 'strength' of the HRM system. *Academy of Management Review*, 29, 2, 203–221.

Brewster, C. and Larsen, H.H. (1992). Human resource management in Europe: evidence from ten countries. *International Journal of Human Resource Management*, 3, 3, 409–433.

Brewster, C., Wood, G., Croucher, R. and Brookes, M. (2007). Collective and individual voice: convergence in Europe? *International Journal of Human Resource Management*, 18, 7, 1246–1262.

Budhwar, P. (2000). Evaluating levels of strategic integration and devolvement of human resource management in the UK. *Personnel Review*, 29, 2, 141–161.

Budhwar, P. and Khatri, N. (2001). HRM in context: applicability of HRM models in India. *International Journal of Cross Cultural Management*, 1, 3, 333–356.

Budhwar, P.S. and Mellahi, K. (2006). *Managing Human Resources in the Middle-East*. Routledge, London.

Collier, P. (2010). The political economy of natural resources. *Social Research*, 77, 4, 1105–1132.

Cunningham, I. and Hyman, J. (1999). Devolving human resource responsibilities to the line: beginning of the end or a new beginning for personnel? *Personnel Review*, 28, 1/2, 9–27.

Darwish, T., Mohamed, A.F., Wood, G., Singh, S. and Fleming, J. (2017). Can HRM alleviate the negative effects of the resource curse on Firms? Evidence from Brunei. *Personnel Review*, 46, 8, 1931–1947.

Darwish, T. and Singh, S. (2013). Does strategic HR involvement and devolvement enhance organisational performance? Evidence from Jordan. *International Journal of Manpower*, 34, 6, 674–692.

Darwish, T., Singh, S. and Mohamed, A.F. (2013). The role of strategic HR practices in organisational effectiveness: an investigation in the country of Jordan. *International Journal of Human Resource Management*, 24, 17, 3343–3362.

Darwish, T., Singh, S. and Wood, G. (2015). The impact of human resource practices on actual and perceived organizational performance in a Middle-Eastern emerging market. *Human Resource Management*, 55, 2, 261–281.

Evans, W.R. and Davis, W.D. (2005). High-performance work systems and organizational performance: the mediating role of internal social structure. *Journal of Management*, 31, 5, 758–775.

Guest, D.E. (1997). Human resource management and performance: a review and research agenda. *International Journal of Human Resource Management*, 8, 3, 263–276.

Guest, D.E. (2011). Human resource management and performance: still searching for some answers. *Human Resource Management Journal*, 22, 1, 3–13.

Haber, S. and Menaldo, V. (2001). Do natural resources fuel authoritarianism? A reappraisal of the resource curse. *American Political Science Review*, 105, 1, 1–26.

Huang, T.C. (2000). Are the human resource practices of effective firms distinctly different from those of poorly performing ones? Evidence from Taiwanese enterprises. *International Journal of Human Resource Management*, 11, 2, 436–451.

Karami, A., Jones, B. and Kakabadse, N. (2008). Does strategic human resource management matter in high-tech sector? Some learning points for SME managers. *Corporate Governance*, 8, 1, 7–17.

Lawler, E.E. (1992). *The Ultimate Advantage: Creating the High Involvement Organization*. Jossey-Bass, San Francisco, CA.

Lawrey, R.N. (2010). An economist's perspective on economic diversification in Brunei Darussalam. *CSPS Strategy and Policy Journal*, 1, 1, 13–28.

Mehlum, H., Moene, K. and Torvik, R. (2006). Institutions and the resource curse. *The Economic Journal*, 116, 508, 1–20.

Mellahi, K. (2007). The effect of regulations on HRM: private sector firms in Saudi Arabia. *The International Journal of Human Resource Management*, 18, 1, 85–99.

Mellahi, K. and Wood, G. (2002). Desperately seeking stability: the making and remaking of the Saudi Arabian petroleum growth regime. *Competition and Change*, 6, 4, 345–362.

Minnis, J.R. (2000). Caught between tradition and modernity: technical and vocational education in Brunei Darussalam. *Journal of Educational Development*, 20, 3, 247–259.

Nuur, C. and Laestadius, S. (2010). Natural resources and old industrialized nations: is there a regional dimension to the resource curse? *The 8th Conference of the EURS Conference*, Vienna, 15–17 September, pp. 1–32.

Paauwe, J. (2009). HRM and performance: achievements, methodological, issues and prospects. *Journal of Management Studies*, 46, 1, 129–142.

Pfeffer, J. (1998). Seven practices of successful organizations. *California Management Review*, 40, 2, 96–124.

Rogers, E. and Wright, P. (1998). Measuring organisational performance in strategic human resource management: problems, prospects, and performance information markets. *Human Resource Management Review*, 8, 3, 311–331.

Ross, M. (2012). *The Oil Curse: How Petroleum Wealth Shapes the Development of Nations*. Princeton University Press, Princeton, NJ.

Santoso, D. (2009). The construction site as a multicultural workplace: a perspective of minority migrant workers in Brunei. *Construction Management and Economics*, 29, 6, 529–537.

Sheehan, M. (2012). Devolvement of HRM and perceived performance within multinational corporations (MNCs). *European Journal of International Management*, 6, 1, 101–127.

Singh, S., Darwish, T. and Anderson, N. (2012a). Strategic intent, high performance HRM, and the role of the HR director: an investigation into attitudes and practices in the country of Jordan. *International Journal of Human Resource Management*, 23, 14, 3027–3044.

Singh, S., Darwish, T., Costa, A.C. and Anderson, N. (2012b). Measuring HRM and organisational performance: concepts, issues, and framework. *Management Decision*, 50, 4, 651–667.

Singh, S., Darwish, T.K. and Potočnik, K. (2016). Measuring organizational performance: a case for subjective measures. *British Journal of Management*, 27, 1, 214–224.

Singh, S., Darwish, T., Wood, G. and Mohamed, A.F. (2017). Institutions, complementarity, human resource management and performance in a South-East Asian Petrostate: the case of Brunei. *The International Journal of Human Resource Management*, 28, 18, 2538–2569.

Singh, S., Wood, G., Darwish, T., Fleming, J. and Mohammed, A.F. (2019). Human resource management in multinational and domestic enterprises: a comparative institutional analysis in Southeast Asia. *Thunderbird International Business Review*, 61, 229–241.

Sullivan, J. (2003). Knocking down the silos. *Human Resource*, March, pp. 16–18.

Tasie, G. (2009). Can Japanese management styles be applied to Africa? *African Journal of Business Management*, 3, 4, 233–239.

The Economic Outlook for Southeast Asia, China and India (2014). Beyond the middle-income trap, available at: doi:10.1787/saeo-2014-en.

Truss, C. and Gratton, L. (1994). Strategic human resource management: a conceptual approach. *International Journal of Human Resource Management*, 5, 3, 663–686.

Truss, C., Gratton, L., Hope-Hailey, V., Mcgovern, P. and Stiles, P. (1997). Soft and hard models of human resource management: a reappraisal. *Journal of Management Studies*, 34, 1, 53–73.

Wiens, D., Poast, P. and Williams, C. (2014). The political resource curse: an empirical re-evaluation. *Political Research Quarterly*, 67, 4, 783–794.

7 The Role of HR Directors in Multinational and Domestic Enterprises

Satwinder Singh, Geoffrey Wood, Tamer K Darwish, Jocelyne Fleming, and Pengiran Muda Abdul Fattaah

Introduction

There is the question pertaining to whether or not context, and the degree to which an organisation is embedded within it, has the potential to predominate formal business roles and structures so as to establish the degree to which an organisation implemented strategic people management (Singh et al., 2019). A wide range of studies present the view that MNEs are specifically more expected to act as 'norm entrepreneurs', establishing and developing new practices that test and confront different ways of doing things (see Bjorkman & Lervik, 2007; Dore, 2008). This could potentially involve a greater number of innovative and strategic methods in regard to HRM (Brewster et al., 2008; Darwish et al., 2017). The point has also been laboured that the presence of a HR Director presents some degree of insight into the importance the organisation attributes to HRM, as well as the overall inclination of organisations to afford HR professionals with a voice in the case of strategic decision-making (Sheehan, 2005; Darwish & Singh, 2013). As a result of their presence at the Board level, it is recognised that HR Directors are better positioned to achieve good alignment in the case of people management strategies and other elements of organisational strategy (Ulrich & Dulebohn, 2017). This may be attained through supporting and further reinforcing the value of the HR function, notably through considering and managing the adjustments of colleagues in relation to strategic direction alongside other functional areas, as well as through the application of their Board-related insight, so as to ensure that the people management practices implemented are those that are seen to be most well aligned with the business's overall strategic direction (Holden, 2001; Darwish et al., 2017). Improved alignment is recognised as being able to achieve the best use of human capital and the development of combined business capacity at a cognitive level (Aoki, 2010). Nonetheless, in the case of some organisations, it remains that HR Directors have been far more successful than others when it comes to securing this type of position (Singh et al., 2019).

Accordingly, this chapter explores whether the depiction of the HR function at the Board level is seen to enable a more innovative and strategic method for HR, or whether this is seen to be more likely in the case of MNEs. It would seem that the former is more closely linked to conventions and local rules, meaning there could be some degree of movement to innovate, particularly in those countries of residence where there is much evolution being witnessed across institutions (Wood et al., 2014). When it comes to providing answers to this question, the generally strategic role afforded to HR Directors in the case of MNEs in comparison to that of their local counterparts is assessed, as are the variations in line with organisational attributes and their overall inclination to delegate strategic functions, drawing out the implications for theory and practice. This work is centred on evidence gathered in the Brunei context, which is recognised as a micro-state with much recognition in the international organisations arena. As an example, in 2013, FDI made up 5.56% of the country's GDP, with a good contribution made in terms of global performance, as was also demonstrated during earlier years (Trading Economics, 2015). This goes some way to showing that the country provides a context where MNE impacts on more wide-ranging practices are then better positioned to be more specifically pronounced.

Although there is a small but nonetheless growing volume of research centred on HR Directors' role and the overall degree of real power they have (Sparrow & Brewster, 2006), it remains that the majority of this has been directed towards mature markets (e.g., Wright, 2008; Peters & Heusinkveld, 2010; Roche & Teague, 2012). Subsequently, this could highlight the fact that, across a number of emerging markets, the most dominant HR model is authoritarian-paternalistic, which therefore eradicates the necessity for the presence of HR professionals at the Board level (Kuruvilla, 1996; Webster & Wood, 2005), restricting the expanse of support. Nonetheless, bigger organisations functioning in developing markets have come to more commonly afford the HR function with a greater degree of importance – from a nominal perspective, if nothing else. This can be explained in various ways: renewed growth in a number of developing markets as a result of high mineral prices has meant organisations have demonstrated significant growth through a number of new opportunities; regulatory complexities, spanning from unbalanced legislation enforcement through to indigenise pressures, meaning professionals with the ability to handle them and accordingly outline appropriate strategies for such management are then seen as required; and lastly, the issues intrinsic to the dependence on low wage-production models are seen to span from poor productivity through to the ease of competitor entry (Singh et al., 2019). The studies available draw comparisons between MNEs' HR practices alongside those of DEs, with the findings implying that the former are better positioned to progress and implement innovative, more strategic HR systems, with the inclusion of influences from both their countries of origin and the emerging global best practice (Brewster et al., 2008; Gooderham et al., 2008; Ferner et al., 2011). Nonetheless, the majority of the studies have directed attention to various bundles of practice rather than to HR strategy-related concerns. As has been emphasised through Business Systems Theory, MNEs are known to encompass institutional domains, which therefore means that they are exposed not only to a number of different challenging institutional pressures but are also not as strongly commanded by the rules and principles identified in a single setting (Whitley, 1999, 2007). Importantly, this means the question of whether or not formal business structures and the presence of a HR Director has overall impacts on the promotion of strategic HRM, or whether it is predominantly an outcome stemming from the environment and the degree of organisational embeddedness within it (Singh et al., 2019). When taking this consideration into account, there is the aim to develop greater insight into host country and home effects. This chapter aims to detail not only their effects on formal business roles and structures but also to investigate how these could be seen to manifest in specific contexts.

The MNE and Local Context: Comparative Institutional Analysis

When it comes to describing the nature of organisations in line with context, comparative institutional analysis is recognised as key (Singh et al., 2019). Nonetheless, a large number of works have centred on the more wide-ranging political economy; this is seen to place additional burdens on those organisations looking to function across a specific context (Hall & Soskice, 2001; Hancke et al., 2007). There has also been the recognised propensity to fail to consider organisations that encompass national settings (see Hall & Soskice, 2001). Nonetheless, as has been noted in the work of Dore (2008), MNEs are, as dictated by their nature, far less solely focused on one context; in this case, they are subject to what may at times be recognised as inconsistent and conflicting pressures from all of the countries in which they function (Singh et al., 2019). Accordingly, this allows a greater expanse to diverge from what has been recognised as normal and instead focus on presenting new and innovative approaches (Dore, 2008). It is in line with this that greater attention has been afforded to MNEs through leading developments in Business Systems Theory (Singh et al., 2019). Owing to the fact that MNEs overlap when it comes to institutional arenas, it is inevitable that country-of-origin pressures will become weakened (Nguyen, 2014). When it comes to entering into new markets, MNEs could aim to implement practices that have been devised in foreign regions, whilst also dealing with pressures to confirm to the local context (Brewster et al., 2008). Of course, it is imperative that this is done if they are to achieve a competitive edge stemming from local production regimes (Whitley,

1999, 2010; Morgan, 2012). Pivotal to the literature on comparative capitalism is complementarity, which is recognised as being an amalgamation of practices and rules that, when brought together, achieve more promising results than would be achieved if not combined (Hall & Soskice, 2001; Whitley, 2010). In an effort to achieve such advantages, there is a need for players to align their practices alongside the leading approaches in recognition of the view that this would be more likely to be the one recognised as best suited to the context (Whitley, 2010). Literature available on capitalism originally maintained that key complementarities could only be experienced in the case of the most well-developed societies, with developing markets seen to be progressing towards one of the leading, more established frameworks (Hall & Soskice, 2001). Work carried out later on has come to acknowledge that the most developed societies are not aligned with a monopolistic approach on complementarity but rather recognise that other markets' complementarities are, to the very best degree, impartial and incomplete, and further aim to satisfy a far smaller team of players than would otherwise be possible in the case of developing markets (Lane & Wood, 2014; Cooke et al., 2017). In the case of the latter, it is most probable that institutional arrangements will be flexible in terms of evolvement, not only in regard to external world market and transnational institution pressures, but also internal actors' opportunism (Wood et al., 2014; Cooke et al., 2017). When considering its significant development, the country of Brunei may be expected to encompass significantly beneficial complementarities; on the other hand, however, there is a need to take into account the unbalanced nature of such development, the problems experienced in developing non-resource-based industries, and when it comes to examining structural obstacles in designing efficient corporate governance configurations (Ross, 2015; Singh et al., 2019).

Nonetheless, in more developing and flexible institutional environments, local complementarities are seen to be more likely to be in the developing stage (Hall & Soskice, 2001; Darwish et al., 2015). In this regard, MNEs are both not as likely to be attracted by such contexts but are also expected to have greater freedom to redesign and shape their practices and rules (Morgan & Kristensen, 2007; Morgan, 2012). In consideration to the local complementarities being at a non-developed state, it is clear that local players are then expected to have a more feeble interest in the present order; this means that they will demonstrate a greater inclination to opt for an alternative or emerging approach (Dore, 2008; Morgan, 2012). Nonetheless, in those settings where weakness or fluidity in formal regulations is evident, informal conventions are then more likely to assume a greater degree of value; in this case, it is less likely that outsiders will be in agreement with them and will then achieve fewer advantages from working with them (Whitley, 2007; Morgan, 2012). This can then mean there will be clear separations, from a practice perspective, when comparing DEs and MNEs, even in the case that the former follows more formalised MNE approaches (Morgan & Kristensen, 2007; Nguyen, 2014).

The HR Director's Role

In consideration to the role of the HR Director, there is very little research, with the typologies of Tyson (1987) and Carrol (1991) providing the first examples of work in this regard. The typology of Tyson (1987) provides three individual frameworks; all of these distinguish between the parts adopted by a HR Director, namely the 'clerk of works' model, which involves the HR Director having no role when it comes to the firm's business and strategic aspects and instead only adopting an administrative role; then there is the 'contract manager' model, where emphasis is placed on trade unions and ensuring insight into and understanding of agreements between the firm and various parties, whilst ensuring everything is done to keep issues at a minimum; and then there is the 'architect' model, which involves the HR Director ensuring the presence and maintenance of a valuable relationship with top-level management staff, in addition to Line Management, in mind of ensuring they are able to shape and have an input in terms of the firm's direction in relation to business and corporate approaches. In the case of the typology presented by Carrol (1991), this further expands upon the work carried out by Tyson and further emphasises the change in the HR Director's role to adopt a more strategic direction; this implies that businesses with such a professional would consider people management under a more fundamental lens. The typology presented by Carrol (1991) further incorporates three roles that HR Directors might be seen to adopt across their firm, namely that of delegator, where Line Managers are used to apply policies, technical experts, where the emphasis of the HR Manager's role is placed on their area of speciality, including HR-specific fields of training and development, recruitment and selection, incentives and rewards, and performance appraisal, for example; and innovator, where the HR Director is then able to assist in decision-making in an effort to overcome key obstacles, including issues with productivity and motivation. One restriction in the case of these typologies is that they could be recognised as epochal, or ahistoric; regardless of the HR Director's official job title, it remains that, in times since passed, a more fluid or strategic approach to the role was common than might otherwise be inferred (see Kaufman, 2007). Moreover, it has also been stated that HRM's strategic approach is far from a recent development but has actually been utilised, in various forms, for more than a century, with mention made by John R. Commons, amongst other labour economists (Kaufman, 2002). When considering the definition of such, it remains that professionals and academics in the field of modern management have failed to consider the real job roles, with much differentiation witnessed between contexts (Kaufman, 2002). Accordingly, it may be important to consider not only the presence of a HR Director but, more specifically, the responsibilities of their role.

In much the same way as all senior HR Managers, there is the potential that HR Directors might not be included when it comes to making decisions of a strategic nature; it could be that managerial intervention in terms of the expertise of the HR Director is of a particularly high level (Singh et al., 2019). This might be apparent through the key emphasis on administrative tasks; HR Managers might be assigned to a middle-man role in relation to staff and management, meaning there is a lack of belonging at the management level (see Watson, 1977; Legge, 1978; Tyson & Fell, 1986). In the work of Truss et al. (2002), discussion has centred on whether Type A HR Directors are afforded with any reason responsibility across their firm, with the scholars arguing that these professionals are as involved as business and strategic decisions as others; Type B HR Directors, on the other hand, are considered to direct their attention to their own specialised area of expertise, implementing a more conventional approach. In a comparable vein, the work of Storey (1992) further posits the view that HR Directors may be divided across different groups, such as in relation to supportive and administrative, and to the strategic (Ulrich 1997). Importantly, the point is made by Schuler and Jackson (2001) that HR Directors' role is fluid and changes, meaning it is more likely to shift between areas.

Central Propositions

MNEs have been highlighted as being more expected to encourage innovative or new practices in their local context when compared with their local peers, which could highlight their contact with more wide-ranging alternative practices, a larger abundance of resources, in addition to pressures stemming from the country of origin (Brewster et al., 2008; Ferner et al., 2011). Importantly, it is recognised that MNEs are well positioned to bring more resources to bear in the development of more complex HR systems, as well as also being more inclined to be restricted by established conventions in their country of residence (Morgan, 2012). Furthermore, as has been highlighted above, when considering the lack of complementarities, organisations in developing regions are not as well positioned to devise and present complex HR systems that exploit and sufficiently utilise contextual regulatory dimensions (Hancke et al., 2007). In a much similar vein, this, combined with a lesser wealth of relevant insight as to what is possible through already tried-and-tested approaches, suggests that MNEs would garner fewer advantages if adopting local practices (Hancke et al., 2007). Accordingly, as argued by Singh et al. (2019), it may be stated that, in consideration to the chance to revolutionise, the lesser pressure to align with expectations and standard practices of people management. Hence, the following proposition is outlined:

Proposition 1: MNEs' HR Directors adopt more strategic roles when compared with local counterparts.

It is recognised that MNEs demonstrate an overlap in terms of institutional domains, and are recognised as being only somewhat rooted in a single one (Morgan, 2012). Despite the fact that this could create additional innovation-based space, the issue pertaining to institutional distance becomes apparent. The latter is seen to include both embedded informal ways and formal rules of practice (Xu & Shenker, 2002; Schwens et al., 2011). Importantly, local employees are expected to possess some wealth of insider knowledge, which would position them as being more able to deal with institutional complications at the host country level, and would further mean they are then more entirely incorporated within local networks that commonly provide recompense for developing markets' institutional deficits (Chakrabarty, 2009; Wood et al., 2014). When considering that emigrants are most likely to be disproportionately represented when examining senior job bands – predominantly on the basis of cross-business and international experience and/or skills (Blunt, 1988; Darwish et al., 2017), it could be that a clearer, a greater pressure to assign more tasks and activities to line managers and junior line managers with a local background, which would therefore position them as well experienced and with sufficient contacts to allow them to effectively carry out their management role in the local area (Singh et al., 2019). Hence, we propose the second proposition:

Proposition 2: *MNEs' HR Directors will show a greater tendency to delegate everyday HR tasks to Line and Junior Managers than that shown by their local counterparts.*

Nonetheless, other environmental aspects might also come into play. As an example, it may be suggested that a significant number of migrant workers present a number of HR-related challenges: there might be gaps in skillsets and training, in addition to issues in communication, and much turnover (Baxter-Reid, 2016; Rodriguez et al., 2017). Nonetheless, one aspect of the resource curse shows that local skills development and training models in the case of those sectors lacking in resources are commonly not considered, meaning the assumption cannot be made that local employees will demonstrate more proficiency (Mellahi & Wood, 2002; Mellahi, 2007; Badeep et al., 2017). In this vein, owing to the fact that positions in the gas and oil sector are viewed as more profitable, a high turnover rate across local staff is expected, with employment in other industries potentially viewed as temporary (Badeep et al., 2017; Darwish et al., 2017). Otherwise stated, the management of local and foreign rank and file staff could both present a number of obstacles, although the assumption cannot be made that one bundle of obstacles is of more concern than another (Singh et al., 2019). Based on the above, the third proposition is devised:

Proposition 3: *The local staff-migrant ratio will not be influential in terms of the strategic role played by the HR Director.*

It could be that the somewhat comparative degree of strategic HR is essentially a purpose of business size, as opposed to whether or not an organisation may be considered an MNE; in the case of the latter, it could be considered a proxy for the former in the context of Brunei (Singh et al., 2019). Bigger organisations are better positioned to have a wealth of resources to facilitate capabilities' development (Brewster et al., 2006). In other words, a HR function that is more proficiently resourced provides HR with the ability to adopt a more wide-ranging cross-business strategic role (Brewster et al., 2002; Bratton & Gold, 2017). Once again, larger organisations could potentially derive advantages from official economies of scale (Brewster et al., 2006), which would enable a greater degree of standardisation across routine practices, thus enabling HR capacity to be freed up and directed towards strategic initiatives (Singh et al., 2019). Accordingly, we propose the fourth proposition:

Proposition 4: *A bigger organisation is more expected to have a HR Director that adopts a strategic role.*

Industry, Company Structure, Objectives and Strategies Pursued by the Firm

The issue of whether or not the role of HR Directors can also be shaped by the respective organisation's industry of operation is lacking research, as is consideration to the organisation's structure, its goals and strategies; nonetheless, all of these could be identified as critical aspects of an organisation that could potentially influence and shape the HR Director's role (Singh et al., 2019). In this vein, the point is made by Kuruvilla (1996) that aspects including nations' industrialisation approaches may be pivotal in establishing unique and varied trends of HR practice; nonetheless, sector-centred dynamics and business strategies, including dominant technologies, cause a number of variations in HR trends (Singh et al., 2019). With this noted, the work presented in this chapter sought to establish the effect of such aspects; throughout the process, a number of valuable findings were achieved. Prior research support further highlights that older staff are more expected to have gathered a more in-depth body of organisation-centred and industry-focused knowledge, insight, wisdom, and skills (Birdi et al., 2008). With this noted, it is also relevant to highlight that a HR Director's gender is also recognised as influential in terms of the role carried out (Singh et al., 2019). Lastly, there is also the change that CEOs that have maintained their position for longer are them more likely to be accurate in their estimation of a firm's overall cognitive ability, which therefore means they better utilise their insight and knowledge, and are better able to identify the possible benefit of its staff (Aoki, 2010).

Context and Data

This empirical work presented in this chapter has been carried out in the context of Brunei, where the oil and gas industry is recognised as responsible for a large majority of the country's national income, with gas and oil production dominating the economy (Mohamed et al., 2013; Darwish et al., 2017). Nonetheless, one of the main goals underpinning Brunei's economic activities is that of diversification, with the country recognising that gas and oil are finite and that there is a need to over-come the resource curse (Auty, 1993). Work carried out more recently drawing a contrast between Asian capitalisms has established a number of important defining aspects inherent in economies in Asia; this helps to present approaches to establishing the way in which Brunei may be seen to be aligned with, and depart from, other business systems and frameworks in Asia (Witt & Redding, 2013, 2014; Fainshmidt et al., 2018). Skill levels and education are recognised as high, with economy size reflecting the same; nonetheless, Brunei continues to be over-reliant on oil and gas to a greater degree than other similar petro-states (Singh et al., 2019). Importantly, although the country is known to benefit from the presence of a sound underpinning infrastructure, it nonetheless con-tinues to have weaknesses, including in terms of high-level infrastruc-ture, such as in regard to healthcare, university, and transport (Singh et al., 2019). Furthermore, when compared alongside Witt & Redding (2013, 2014)'s taxonomy of key institutional features that showcase var-ious economies in Asia, Brunei is recognised as being more compara-ble with less developed Asian economies than developed ones (Michael, 2018; Singh et al., 2017; c.f. Fainschmidt et al., 2018).

Data gathered for the work presented in this chapter has been col-lected following the completion of a survey utilising a sample of HR Directors completing their roles at Domestic and Multinational Enter-prises in the Brunei context. When examining the domestic and for-eign organisations in operation in the country, a total count of 465 was made. Subsequently, a total random sample size of 214 was selected. A total of 151 replies were received, notably 60% (n = 88) from DEs and 40% (n = 63) from MNEs, therefore achieving a response rate of 70%

which is adequate to achieve the comparative nature of this work (for more details in relation to measurement, data and analysis, see Singh et al., 2019).

Discussion and Conclusions

MNEs are generally expected to have more proficiently developed HR systems than their local counterparts, as highlighted by Budhwar (2000). Nonetheless, when drawing a contrast between organisations with HR representation at the Board level, key differences were identified: HR Directors in MNEs were seen to have a greater tendency to play a strategic role in their firm when compared with their peers (Singh et al., 2019). This could be explained first by considering that MNEs are more likely than domestic organisations to be exposed to global best practices; second, MNEs are generally only somewhat embedded in a single environment and are required to face not only home and host country institutions but also are seen to have a greater range of strategic options and more autonomy when compared with their locally operating competitors (Singh et al., 2019). Despite the fact that the Board-level HR function could communicate greater prominence (Lawler & Mohrman, 2003), this is not to say that a strategic role is being carried out. In actual fact, it could be that the latter actually signifies an outcome pertaining to the density of the relationship network across a firm, as well as between it and other parties (Hall & Soskice, 2001; Hancke et al., 2007). When organisations are recognised as embedded in only a single environment, it is possible that senior management generally and HR Directors in particular could have a greater degree of flexibility and independence to innovate and assign a more strategic-based approach to the HR role than might otherwise be recognised as normal in any specific context (Singh et al., 2019). ·

The work presented in this chapter has arrived at conclusions that allow for further insight into host and home country pressures on MNEs and the more generalised HR function. Despite the fact that studies on international HRM has been far more specifically focused on HR practice variations in line with host and home country dynamics, as shown in numerous works (Brewster et al., 2008; Gooderham et al., 2008; Ferner et al., 2011), this chapter delivers greater understanding into the key impacts of adopting a multinational nature across a firm; the HR Director's role is seen to be far more strategic in those businesses that extend across national boundaries (Singh et al., 2019).

It was found through this work that, when examining MNEs' proficiency compared with their local peers, there is very little difference in the tendency of HR Directors to assign their formalised and routine tasks to other individuals; however, DEs were recognised as both implementing a strategic-based method for HRM but also were found to be more on-board with delegation; this could be seen to signify some degree of incapacity to differentiate between routine and strategic HR functions (Singh et al., 2019). On the other hand, informal networks and ties functioning beyond formal regulatory models could enable and accordingly orchestrate communication between employees at varying authoritarian levels both beyond and across the organisations in developing market environments (Wood et al., 2010). There is then the likelihood that local staff will be more aware and have a greater insight into local realities and what may be viewed as practical; otherwise stated, should MNEs be seen to be better positioned to pursue innovation, they might not be as adept at encouraging more decentralised approaches than their local peers, even in the case of their own organisations; this could further highlight limitations in regard to any evangelising role (Singh et al., 2019).

In the empirical work presented in this chapter only a very small body of support was garnered to reinforce the view that the organisational structure, aims and approaches implemented by the firm have any degree of influence on the HR Director's role across the firm; that is to say that adopting a strategic role is not only a function of complexity, as would be the case amongst multinational firms; however, the latter does highlight a valuable path for exploration (Singh et al., 2019). This could emphasis small countries' more wide-ranging extent of homogeneity; organisations in varying sectors might be more inclined to adopt roles in close spatial proximity, with fewer regional differences witnessed when examining institutional effects (c.f. Maskell & Malmberg, 1999; Lane & Wood, 2014).

Implications for Practice

The work presented in this chapter validates the value of MNEs in terms of revolutionising more combined and modern methods of HRM, as well as the various limitations in regard to the degree to which they might affect their local peers. Should local organisations formally assign HR Directors with Board representation, they will then be not as inclined to afford a strategic role. As argued by Singh et al. (2019), although fundamental aspects of MNEs' HR practice has been profoundly shaped by national legislation, such as in regard to ensuring compliance with equal opportunities and in terms of recruitment legislation, it remains that there is ongoing differentiation when examining areas of practice not subject to formal regulation; more specifically, this emphasises that the HR Director role is active and lived, with a disconnect apparent in relation to normal status and how it functions from a practical standpoint; contexts and firms not familiar with HR beyond any essential role will not always be open to applying a more strategic focus, regardless of whether or not the Board level communicates such a desire. Solving historical marginalisation essentially warrants incremental negotiation alongside fundamental actors. With HR Directors being based abroad or originating from abroad, outsiders are then expected to experience problems in ensuring the compliance of local employees with new HR Directions and the support of such; at times, this can go some way to describing a more wide-ranging degree of compliance and will facilitate new HR directions; this can then go some way to explaining a more pronounced tendency towards centralisation (Singh et al., 2019). Nonetheless, it is not likely that the latter will implement any changes outside of the borders of clear directives.

Despite the recognition that HRM is acknowledged as beneficial to a large number of firms, it would appear that the opportunities are far more vast in the case of multinational firms, as well as when there is a weaker attraction of practices and local institutions; in this case, in those contexts where informal norms and established regulations are not as fluid or are less embedded, innovation is seen to be more problematic, as well as where the organisation is seen to be more intimately linked to existing players (Singh et al., 2019). The degree to which HR Directors are able to achieve a difference highlights not only skills in dealing with more intricate issues (Truss et al., 2002), but, in addition, the opportunities and relative space provided by a specific socio-economic and business-related context (Darwish et al., 2017; Singh et al., 2019).

Future Work

The work presented in this chapter has drawn a comparison between MNEs and their local counterparts, though notably emphasis has not been directed towards contrasting organisations with HR Directors and those without. As argued by Singh et al. (2019), it would therefore be valuable to complete a work centred on the latter, highlighting greater differences; regardless, however, it would appear that, should there be a HR Director in a firm, the general degree to which a strategic role is followed depends on the whether or not the organisation is multinational. At once, a more in-depth examination as to the differences in formal HR structures and roles provide a solid foundation for future investigation.

The work presented in this chapter is the first of its kind, notably completed in an emerging country with a significant abundance of large-scale MNEs; a country where MNEs are not so commonplace could be seen to be linked with a greater pressure to fit in and for HR practices to be more intimately aligned with those of local peers (Singh et al., 2019). Once again, a more in-depth understanding of the numerous determinants and the differing nature pertaining to MNEs' local embeddedness could be achieved through the completion of a comparative dimension, analysing a more encompassing range of Asian states; one additional work could focus on investigating country-of-origin effects in relation to HR Directors and the type of role they adopt (Singh et al., 2019).

References

Aoki, M. (2010). *Corporations in Evolving Diversity*. Oxford, England: Oxford University Press.

Auty, R. (1993). Sustaining Development in Mineral Economies: The resource curse thesis. Routledge, London, England.

Badeeb, R. A., Lean, H. H., & Clark, J. (2017). The evolution of the natural resource curse thesis: A critical literature survey. *Resources Policy*, 51, 123–134.

Baxter-Reid, H. (2016). Buying into the 'good worker' rhetoric or being as good as they need to be? The effort bargaining process of new migrant workers. *Human Resource Management Journal*, 26, 3, 337–350.

Birdi, K., Clegg, C., Patterson, M., Robinson, A., Stride, C., Wall, T., & Wood, S. (2008). The impact of human resource and operational management practices on company productivity: A longitudinal study. *Personnel Psychology*, 61, 467–501.

Bjorkman, I., & Lervik, J. E. (2007). Transferring HR practices within multinational corporations. *Human Resource Management Journal*, 17, 4, 320–335.

Blunt, P. (1988). Cultural consequences for organization change in a Southeast Asian state: Brunei. *The Academy of Management Executive*, 2, 3, 235–240.

Bratton, J., & Gold, J. (2017). *Human resource management: Theory and practice*. London: Palgrave.

Brewster, C., Wood, G., & Brookes, M. (2008). Similarity, isomorphism and duality? Recent survey evidence on the HRM policies of MNCs. *British Journal of Management*, 19, 4, 320–342.

Brewster, C., Wood, G., Brookes, M., & Ommeren, J. V. (2006). What determines the size of the HR function? A cross-national analysis. *Human Resource Management*, 45, 1, 3–21.

Budhwar, P. (2000). Evaluating levels of strategic integration and devolvement of human resource management in the UK. *Personnel Review*, 29, 2, 141–161.

Carroll, S. J. (1991). The new HRM roles, responsibilities, and structures. In R. S. Schuler (Ed.), *Managing human resources in the information age* (pp. 204–226). Washington, DC: Bureau of National Affairs.

Chakrabarty, S. (2009). The influence of national culture and institutional voids on family ownership of large firms: A country level empirical study. *Journal of International Management*, 15, 1, 32–45.

Cooke, F., Veen, A., & Wood, G. (2016). What do we know about cross-country comparative studies in HRM? A critical review of literature in the period of 2000–2014. *International Journal of Human Resource Management*, 28, 1, 196–233.

Darwish, T. K., Mohamed, A. F., Wood, G., Singh, S., & Fleming, J. (2017). Can HRM alleviate the negative effects of the resource curse on firms? Evidence from Brunei. *Personnel Review*, 46, 8, 1931–1947.

Darwish, T. K., & Singh, S. (2013). Does strategic HR involvement and devolvement enhance organisational performance? Evidence from Jordan. *International Journal of Manpower*, 34, 6, 674–692.

Darwish, T. K., Singh, S., & Wood, G. (2015). The impact of human resource practices on actual and perceived organizational performance in a Middle-Eastern emerging market. *Human Resource Management*, 55, 2, 261–281.

Dore, R. (2008). Best practice winning out? *Socio-Economic Review*, 6, 4, 779–784.

Fainshmidt, S., Judge, W. Q., Aguilera, R. V., & Smith, A. (2016). Varieties of institutional systems: A contextual taxonomy of understudied countries. *Journal of World Business*, 53, 3, 307–322.

Ferner, A., Tregaskis, O., Edwards, P., Edwards, T., Marginson, P., Adam, D., & Meyer, M. (2011). HRM structures and subsidiary discretion in foreign multinationals in the UK. *International Journal of Human Resource Management*, 22, 3, 483–509.

Gooderham, P., Fenton-o'creevy, M., & Nordhaug, O. (2008). Human resource management in US subsidiaries in Europe: Centralization or autonomy? *Journal of International Business Studies*, 39, 1, 151–166.

Hall, P., & Soskice, D. (2001). An Introduction to the varieties of capitalism. In P. Hall & D. Soskice (Eds.), *Varieties of capitalism: The institutional basis of competitive advantage* (pp. 1–68). Oxford, England: Oxford University Press.

Hancke, B., Rhodes, M., & Thatcher, M. (2007). Introduction. In B. Hancke, M. Rhodes, & M. Thatcher (Eds.), *Beyond varieties of capitalism: Conflict, contradiction, and complementarities in the European economy* (pp. 3–38). Oxford, England: Oxford University Press.

Hofstede, G. (2001). *Culture's consequences*. Thousand Oaks, CA: Sage Publications.

Holden, R. (2001). Managing people's values and perceptions in multi-cultural organisations: The experience of an HR director. *Employee Relations*, 23, 6, 614–626.

Kaufman, B. E. (2002). The theory and practice of strategic HRM and participative management: Antecedents in early industrial relations. *Human Resource Management Review*, 11, 4, 505–533.

Kaufman, B. E. (2007). The development of HRM in historical and international perspective. In P. Boxall & J. Purcell (Eds.), *Oxford handbook of human resource management* (pp. 19–47). Oxford, England: Oxford University Press.

Kuruvilla, S. (1996). National industrialization strategies and their influence on patterns of HR practices. *Human Resource Management Journal*, 6, 3, 22–41.

Lane, C., & Wood, G. (2014). Capitalist diversity: Work and employment relations. In A. Wilkinson, G. Wood, & R. Deeg (Eds.), *Oxford handbook of employment relations: Comparative employment systems* (pp. 156–172). Oxford, England: Oxford University Press.

Lawler, E. E., & Mohrman, S. A. (2003). HR as a strategic partner: What does it take to make it happen? *Human Resource Planning*, 26, 3, 15–29.

Mani, A. (2008). A century of contributions by Indians in Negara Brunei Darussalam. In K. Kevasapany, A. Mani, & P. Ramasamy (Eds.), *Rising India and Indian Communities in East Asia* (pp. 171–194). Singapore: ISEAS.

Maskell, P., & Malmberg, A. (1999). Localised learning and industrial competitiveness. *Cambridge Journal of Economics*, 23, 2, 167–185.

Mellahi, K. (2007). The effect of regulations on HRM: Private sector firms in Saudi Arabia. *International Journal of Human Resource Management*, 18, 1, 85–99.

Mellahi, K., & Wood, G. (2002). Desperately seeking stability: The making and remaking of the Saudi Arabian petroleum growth regime. *Competition and Change*, 6, 4, 345–362.

Michael, B. (2018). What does Brunei teach us about using Human Development Index rankings as a policy tool? *Development Policy Review*, 36, S1, 414–431.

Mohamed, A. F., Singh, S., Irani, Z., & Darwish, T. K. (2013). An analysis of recruitment, training and retention practices in domestic and multinational enterprises in the country of Brunei Darussalam. *The International Journal of Human Resource Management*, 24, 10, 2054–2081.

Morgan, G. (2012). International business, multinationals and national business systems. In G. Wood & M. Demirbag (Eds.), *Handbook of institutional approaches to international business* (pp. 18–40). Cheltenham, England: Edward Elgar.

Morgan, G., & Kristensen, P. H. (2006). The contested space of multinationals: Varieties of institutionalism, varieties of capitalism. *Human Relations*, 59, 11, 1467–1490.

Nguyen, Q. T. K. (2014). The regional Strategies of British multinational subsidiaries in South East Asia. *British Journal of Management*, 25, S1, S60–S76.

Peters, P., & Heusinkveld, S. (2010). Institutional explanations for managers' attitudes towards telehome working. *Human Relations*, 63, 1, 107–135.

Roche, W. K., & Teague, P. (2012). Business partners and working the pumps: Human resource managers in the recession. *Human Relations*, 65, 10, 1333–1358.

Rodriguez, J. K., Johnstone, S., & Procter, S. (2017). Regulation of work and employment: Advances, tensions and future directions in research in international and comparative HRM. *International Journal of Human Resource Management*, 28, 21, 2957–2982.

Ross, M. L. (2015). What have we learned about the resource curse? *Annual Review of Political Science*, 18, 239–259.

Santoso, D. S. (2009). The construction site as a multicultural workplace: A perspective of minority migrant workers in Brunei. *Construction Management and Economics*, 27, 6, 529–537.

Schuler, R. S., & Jackson, S. E. (2001). HR issues and activities in mergers and acquisitions. *European Management Journal*, 19, 3, 239–253.

Schwens, C., Eiche, J., & Kabst, R. (2011). The moderating impact of informal institutional distance and formal institutional risk on SME entry mode choice. *Journal of Management Studies*, 48, 2, 330–351.

Sheehan, C. (2005). A model for HRM strategic integration. *Personnel Review*, 34, 2, 192–209.

Singh, S., Darwish, T. K., Wood, G., & Mohamed, A. F. (2017). Institutions, complementarity, human resource management and performance in a South-East Asian Petrostate: The case of Brunei. *The International Journal of Human Resource Management*, 28, 18, 2538–2569.

Singh, S., Wood, G., Darwish, T., Fleming, J., & Mohammed, A.F. (2019). Human resource management in multinational and domestic enterprises: A comparative institutional analysis in Southeast Asia. *Thunderbird International Business Review*, 61, 229–241.

Sparrow, P., & Brewster, C. (2006). Globalizing HRM: The growing revolution in managing employees internationally. In C. Cooper & R. Burke

(Eds.), *The human resources revolution: Research and practice* (pp. 99–122). London, England: Elsevier.

Storey, J. (1992). *Developments in the management of human resources.* Oxford, England: Blackwell Publishing.

Trading Economics (2015). *Brunei Foreign Director Investment* (World Bank Data). Retrieved from http://www.theglobaleconomy.com/Brunei/Foreign_Direct_Investment

Truss, C., Gratton, L., Hope-Hailey, V., Stiles, P., & Zaleska, J. (2002). Paying the piper: Choice and constraint in changing HR functional roles. *Human Resource Management Journal*, 12, 2, 39–63.

Tyson, S. (1987). The management of the personnel function. *Journal of Management Studies*, 24, 5, 523–532.

Tyson, S., & Fell, A. (1986). *Evaluating the personnel function.* London, England: Hutchinson.

Ulrich, D. (1997). *Human resource champions: The next agenda for adding value and delivering results.* Boston, MA: Harvard Business School.

Ulrich, D., & Dulebohn, J. H. (2015). Are we there yet? What's next for HR? *Human Resource Management Review*, 25, 2, 188–204.

Watson, T. J. (1977). *The personnel managers.* London, England: Routledge & Kegan Paul.

Webster, E., & Wood, G. (2005). Human resource management practice and institutional constraints. *Employee Relations*, 27, 4, 369–385.

Whitley, R. (1999). *Divergent capitalisms: The social structuring and change of business systems.* Oxford, England: Oxford University Press.

Whitley, R. (2007). *Business systems and organizational capabilities.* Oxford, England: Oxford University Press.

Whitley, R. (2010). Changing competition in market economies. In G. Morgan, J. Campbell, C. Crouch, O. Pedersen, & R. Whitley (Eds.), *The Oxford handbook of comparative institutional analysis* (pp. 363–398). Oxford, England: Oxford University Press.

Witt, M. A., & Redding, G. (2013). Asian business systems: Institutional comparison, clusters and implications for varieties of capitalism and business systems theory. *Socio-Economic Review*, 11, 2, 265–300.

Witt, M. A., & Redding, G. (2014). Introduction. In M. A. Witt & G. Redding (Eds.), *The Oxford handbook of Asian business systems* (pp. 1–8). Oxford, England: Oxford University Press.

Wood, G., Dibben, P., & Ogden, S. (2014). Comparative capitalism without capitalism, and production without workers: The limits and possibilities of contemporary institutional analysis. *International Journal of Management Reviews*, 16, 4, 384–396.

Wood, G., Dibben, P., Stride, C., & Webster, E. (2010). HRM in Mozambique: Homogenization, path dependence or segmented business system? *Journal of World Business*, 46, 1, 31–41.

Wright, C. (2008). Reinventing human resource management: Business partners, internal consultants and the limits to professionalization. *Human Relations*, 61, 8, 1063–1086.

Xu, D., & Shenkar, O. (2002). Note: Institutional distance and the multinational enterprise. *Academy of Management Review*, 27, 4, 608–618.

8 Recruitment, Training, and Retention Practices

Do Domestic Firms Differ from Multinationals?

Pengiran Muda Abdul Fattaah,
Satwinder Singh, and Tamer K Darwish

Introduction

One of the most important aspects that influence organisational success is the recruitment, training, and retention of employees, and how such processes are carried out (Mohamed et al., 2013; Singh et al., 2019). This link, which presents the foundation underpinning the potential to garner and maintain a competitive edge against rival companies operating in the same domain, has been the focus of much study and examination by business economists (see, for example, Baron, 1988; Milgrom, 1988; Appelbaum and Batt, 1994; Darwish et al., 2017). Accordingly, empirical analyses in this field is now receiving much more attention and research effort considering its applied value within the business world, as well as the potential to arrive at new and valuable findings (Mohamed et al., 2013). When reviewing the empirical works in this field, some can be identified as having been carried out in the multinational enterprises' (MNEs) context, with much focus centred on drawing comparisons between human resources management (HRM) practices across MNE subsidiaries in the context of emerging economies (see, for example, Guest and Hoque, 1996; Boxall et al., 2007; Haak-Saheem et al., 2016). With this noted, this chapter seeks to provide a contribution to the literature through the completion of a research conducted in a comparable vein, in the context of a non-Western, developing economy. Moreover, this chapter presents a direct comparison pertaining to the HR practices implemented throughout the recruitment, training, and retention processes (from here referred to as HR practices) in the specific domain of domestic enterprises (DEs) and multinational enterprises (MNEs). As is commonly acknowledged, MNEs are viewed as being fundamental players in the arena of global commerce, and are, as a result, are rapidly positioning themselves as pivotal in economic development (Singh et al., 2019). This chapter, accordingly, presents an effort in this direction in completing a study in the context of Brunei. It seeks to satisfy four research questions: first, are the criteria adopted by MNEs with regard to recruitment, training and retention more detailed and thorough than those in DEs?; second, when considering their global operationality, do MNEs seek to ensure superior internal continuity through the presence of smooth executive succession and promotion?; third, does a comparison across DEs and MNEs highlight any differences in terms of turnover rates?; and fourth, does an organisation's age and size influence the overall operation of the three considerations under exploration and examination in the current chapter?

The following section provides a summarised overview of the literature available on the three HR practices, and further discusses the hypotheses outlined following on from the literature review. The chapter ends with discussion and conclusions.

Recruitment and Selection

The issue of staffing, notably comprising recruitment and selection, has been acknowledged as being a key strategic international HRM (IHRM) practice by MNEs with the aim of ensuring smooth global operations, coordination, and control (Dowling and Schuler, 1990; Hendry, 1994; Sparrow et al., 1994; Haak-Saheem et al., 2016; Singh et al., 2017). In overseas operation, a key challenge faced by MNEs is to match appropriate staff with job specifications that might differ from affiliate to affiliate (Shen and Edwards, 2004; Darwish et al., 2017).

Another fundamental recruitment and selection consideration pertains to whether such firms opt to recruit on an internal or external basis (Mohamed et al., 2013). Should the organisation make the decision to recruit externally, there are a number of different possibilities open to MNEs, such as recruiting from the home country, the host country, a third country, or any combination of such (Scullion, 1995). Four different methods of international staffing, namely the ethnocentric (home country nationals filling key positions); geocentric (ensuring the recruitment of the most suitable individual for the role, regardless of nationality); the polycentric (home country nationals adopting roles in running corporate headquarters whilst host country nationals run 'foreign' subsidiaries); and finally, the regiocentric method (division of operations into geographic sectors, by MNEs, with the staff accordingly divided between such sectors) come into play (Perlmutter, 1969; Dowling et al., 1999).

When considering recruitment and selection on a per-company basis, much variation has been witnessed in line with country of origin (Singh et al., 2019); for instance, in the case of British organisations, recruitment agencies and executive search consultants are commonly utilised in the filling of managerial role; this is not, however, necessarily witnessed across Asian organisations, as noted by Hsu and Leat (2000). Haak-Saheem et al. (2016) have also reported mixed results in relation to recruitment and selection practices from a sample of MNEs located in the Gulf region. Thus, in line with the discussion presented so far, we propose the following:

H1: In consideration to MNEs' international operations, such entities would be more likely to adopt more rigorous recruitment criteria when compared with DEs.

H2: In consideration to the greater scope of choice made available to MNEs, there is a greater tendency amongst such organisations to depend on external recruitment when seeking to fill roles than the tendency displayed by DEs.

Internal career opportunities availability has the potential to safeguard estrangement chance from increasing, as this is recognised as potentially arising when individuals are recruited externally to fill senior roles (Noe et al., 2006; Singh et al., 2017). Furthermore, the presence of such opportunities further helps to guarantee that those adopting role transfer in order to fill a vacant position have understanding of the firm and the role they are set to fill (Pfeffer, 1994). Importantly, ensuring there are opportunities available, from an internal perspective, has also been recognised as positively associated with market share, investment and perceived profits, as highlighted in the work of Verburg, (1998), Darwish et al. (2016) and Singh et al. (2017) Moreover, in terms of cross-national or cross-cultural comparison works, there has been a lack of clarity in the findings. As an example, it has been determined in the study of Ferner et al. (2001) that German MNEs operating in Spain and the United Kingdom exported German characteristics; this further comprised their long-term positioning in the organisations. The work of Glinow et al. (1999) has established that a number of differences form a cross-cultural perspective emerge when comparing Asian with European promotion criteria, notably recognised as being stemming from differences outlined in Hofstede's cultural values. For instance, inclusion of high-level collectivism in the Taiwanese context, where much importance is directed towards seniority when contrasted alongside the experience and performance of staff in organisations in the United Kingdom. Accordingly, this has resulted in the following hypothesis being outlined:

H3: When contrasted alongside DEs, MNEs' application of promotion criteria would be far more rigid.

Training Practices

Training practices, as a HR practice, are recognised as having a positive influence on the overall performance and motivation of employees, as documented in various works (Harel and Tzafrir, 1999; Way, 2002; Winterton, 2007; Darwish et al., 2016). The setting within which a firm is able to operate is acknowledged as having a potentially significant effect on the formalised training approaches implemented in firms (Mohamed et al., 2013; Singh et al., 2019). As an example, it is well-accepted that such training initiatives in the United Kingdom are predominantly market-focused, with emphasis placed on job-related skills. In the context of Germany, however, training systems commonly adopt a different form, prioritising job-specific and general-purpose skills. Such a key difference can be seen to be emphasised in the work of McGaughey and De Cieri (1999) and de Guzman et al. (2011), with both highlighting that convergence is being demonstrated by businesses when considering macro-level variables, although such firms are continuing to uphold a degree of variation in regard to micro-level variables. In this regard, McPherson and Roche (1997), for example, have further emphasised the value of training within MNEs, not only in relation to expatriates but also for host country nationals; this is highlighted in mind of achieving progression in international experience, thereby enhancing the overall skill and potential of international employees. Importantly, Cully (1999) carried out an empirical study, which targeted Taiwanese organisations and accordingly established that offer a greater degree of on-the-job training initiatives and schemes when contrasted alongside firms operating in the United Kingdom.

Various works have established a positive link between foreign ownership and training (Shen and Darby, 2006; Zheng et al., 2006). Furthermore, MNEs' tendency to invest in host countries is also seen to comprise human capital investment, notably through training, which is focused on providing a greater degree of return on investment (Lynch and Black, 1995; Darwish et al., 2016). Essentially, international trade requirements further position firms in line with the need to accept higher standards in order to ensure foreign markets are satisfied, with each one different from one the others, with such organisations also needing to be able to accommodate and manage challenges from their competing firms. In line with this viewpoint, we also propose the following:

H4: When compared with DEs, MNEs consider training to be more important.

Retention Practices

The retention practices implemented by organisations seek to manage and overcome the issue pertaining to staff turnover, with the likelihood and opportunity of a firm to do so being dictated by the retention incentives adopted by the firm, in addition to the firm's overall inclination and willingness to implement them (Maertz and Campion, 1998; Mohamed et al., 2013). Such incentives may also be associated with other practices, including selection and training, and internal career opportunities, predominantly owing to the fact that retention capacity is seen to be inherent within such practices, as noted by Reiche (2008). As an example,

Shaw et al. (1998) emphasise the value to be garnered through sufficient pay and benefits when it comes to motivating and attracting employees to remain with the firm; performance-based rewards are also posited as being useful in this regard, as noted by Coff (1997), in addition to a sense of belonging in the firm and possession through stock ownership and profit-sharing. It is noted by Magner et al. (1996) that a greater degree of involvement in the decision-making of a firm can subsequently result in a drop in employee turnover rate. When it comes to considering multinational subsidiaries in particular, the tendency for subsidiaries to implement the HR practices adopted by their headquarters is identified in the work of Harzing and Sorge (2003). It is held that this could potentially induce problematic obstacles as a result of the various settings in which such firms function. Home country-based pressures, in combination with influences of the host country, could also potentially influence the acceptance of the transferred HR practices. Accordingly, there could be some degree of conflict between the two influences, which could then affect the HR practices' overall effectiveness and efficiency (Hofstede, 1998; Miller et al., 2001). In consideration to such difficulties, there are problems in asserting, *a priori*, exactly what the effect of HR practices amongst MNEs could be in terms of employee turnover. In consideration to this, the following hypothesis is detailed in line with the commonly held view in developing economies that, when taking into account greater benefits and higher salaries, MNEs demonstrate a lower employee turnover rate when compared with DEs:

H5: A lower employee turnover rate is recognised amongst MNEs than in DEs.

An organisation's age and size may also influence the choice of HR practices adopted by businesses. A number of different works carried out thus far (see, for example, Van Smoorenburg and Van der Velden, 2000; Tan, 2001) make the statement that variations across HR practices are as a result of organisational size. In the studies of Matlay (1997) and Szamosi et al. (2004), for example, there is reference made to the view that returns on training are more likely to be achieved across larger organisations as a result of the fact that smaller organisations tend to adopt more risk-averse behaviours, which ultimately promotes a lack of future planning and cost-cutting. In consideration to such findings, the following hypothesis is formulated:

H6: The age and size of an organisation is influential in terms of the HR practices adopted by both MNEs and DEs.

Importantly, it is noteworthy to recognise that the hypotheses devised in this work are predominantly centred on the literature review completed in this chapter; they are, to some degree, also based on a general appreciation of the way in which MNEs function in host countries. As an example, it is widely acknowledged throughout the business literature that there are three basic characteristics identifiable in MNEs: first, they must operate in such a way that is considered to be responsive to various environmental factors, whether these are customers, competitors, financial institutions, governments or suppliers; second, when considering their worldwide operation network, there is a common pool of resources at the disposal of an MNE, including assets, human resources, information and patents; and third, a common strategic vision is recognised as the factor linking together MNEs (Rugman and Collinson, 2009). Importantly, the way in which MNEs operate, on an international scale, are recognised as being influenced and guided by such traits, with the practices under the spotlight of examination presented in this chapter treated in a similar vein. Data for this work was generated from a primary survey administered amongst the HR Directors in all companies operating in all sectors in the country of Brunei Darussalam. 151 companies were reached (88 were from DEs and 63 were from MNEs). The latter has greatly helped in achieving the comparative nature of this particular work (for more details in relation to measurement, data, and analysis, see Mohamed et al., 2013).

Discussion and Conclusions

As stated earlier, the objective of this chapter was centred on exploring and examining the behavioural differences identifiable in the recruitment, training, and retention practices of multinational enterprises in comparison with domestic enterprises in the country context of Brunei Darussalam. In line with the survey of available and related literature, combined with already held knowledge of and insight into this topic, a number of hypotheses were devised and detailed, with MNEs recognised as most likely to adopt a greater degree of rigidity and rigor in their recruitment and training methods. Following the completion of the work presented in this chapter, the hypotheses were found to be validated. Moreover, it was also established that, in consideration to firm age, younger organisations – where 'younger' is seen to pertain to those entities of no more than ten years since established – are more likely to be implement a greater degree of stringency in their practices when compared with older, larger organisations; such findings, with certainty, provide further validation as to the view that the three HR practices adopted by MNEs, as discussed in this chapter, are fundamental and of notable value (Mohamed et al., 2013). Furthermore, the findings emphasise the degree of development and progression (Rowley and Benson, 2002; Mohamed et al., 2013). Importantly, some of the findings can be more accurately highlighted when examining HR practices on an individual basis; the differences recognised between MNEs and DEs in relation to recruitment and selection may be owing to differences across firms, as well as potentially owing to globalisation as a whole (Mohamed et al., 2013; Singh et al., 2019). Such dissimilarities may also be recognised in the research conducted by Huang (2000), although notably through the lens of an Eastern context as opposed to Western, with the scholar arriving at findings to show key differences in the majority of HR practices, including career path design, training and staffing, when comparing Western MNEs with organisations operating in the East, including domestic Taiwanese organisations. In the work presented in this chapter, it is recognised that there is a shortfall demonstrated by DEs. In the literature on HRM, focus adopted by many academics and scholars has centred on contingency or universalistic approaches when examining HR practices. Importantly, the universalistic approach is known to encompass an ideal group of 'best practices'; these are intended to provide consistently superior performance at the business level, irrespective of the industry and organisational circumstance, whereas the point is made by the contingency theory that HR practices will also depend on the context, circumstances of the firm, and the environment in which it operates, with all of these factors influential but able to be influenced themselves (Ayentimi et al., 2018; Zhu and Warner, 2019). Importantly, the findings garnered in this work further support the view adopted by the contingency approach as opposed to the best practices approach. It may be inferred that the HR practices implemented across DEs vary and are lacking when compared with those applied in MNEs, with such a difference potentially attributed to the effects of the non-Western cultural context, in addition to any other factors influencing or otherwise shaping the circumstances of DEs in the Brunei context (Mohamed et al., 2013; Singh et al., 2019). These findings may be taken to infer that the HR practices examined and presented in this chapter should not only be viewed as best practice, irrespective of the industry or environment, as highlighted by various scholars.

Moreover, it is possible that there are other factors underpinning the fact that MNEs' emphasis on internal recruitment is supported by this work, rather than DEs. One potential explanation may be the quality of the workforce hired by the domestic firms. Importantly, the quality of the domestic workforce might not be considered to be high in the view of MNEs; internal recruitment might also suggest the placement of expatriates within higher positions in a firm so as to facilitate the smooth supervision of operations (Mohamed et al., 2013; Haak-Saheem and Brewster, 2017). MNEs' use of expatriates echo that which is highlighted in the studies of Shen and Edwards (2004) and Haak-Saheem, and Brewster (2017), who determined expats as being used to ensure international activities coordination and the control of such, as well as supervising and managing the administrative and financial aspects of the firm, in addition to subsidiary operations. One further explanation for the difference identified between MNEs and DEs is the host country's culture: for instance, should there by a high degree of collectivism inherent in the host country, such cultured could then show a preference for internal labour due to the fact it encourages organisational loyalty (Budhwar and Khatri, 2001). Owing to the fact that internal recruitment is vulnerable in terms of differences between cultures, there may be a need for MNEs to make adjustments in line with the domestic setting.

The findings achieved throughout the course of this work further validate the suggested hypotheses in line with training methods, and despite the fact that statistical differences in regard to the importance of such is seen to be greater across MNEs, it remains that the results highlighting the value of DEs' training is similarly high. This emphasises that both DEs and MNEs consider employee training to be of high importance (Mohamed et al., 2013). Moreover, when considering informal training approaches rather than more formalised methods (Wright et al., 2002), it would appear that the former are commonly implemented by both types of organisation. This finding echoes those derived from convergence hypotheses; in addition, the findings may also be seen to be more indirectly aligned with the results of those who emphasised some degree of concern in regard to the quality and suitability of training initiatives when administered on an external basis (see, for example, Zheng et al., 2007). It would appear that the advantages to be garnered through training and of relevance to organisational performance, particularly in the Asian context (see, for example, Osman-Gani and Jacobs, 2005; Jaw et al., 2006; Bao and Analoui, 2011; Singh et al., 2017), could be recognised as enhancing the implementation of more informal, commonly applied training approaches. When considering the results on training approaches being recognised as significantly higher for MNEs could be explained in such a way so as to reflect a defeatist culture, which is, at times, found to be characteristics of small host countries; in addition, it could be that the need to compete with MNEs may prove to be too overwhelming for DEs, thus meaning the latter are discouraged from directing their attention towards training their workforce for fear that MNEs may ultimately adopt poaching tactics (Moahmed et al., 2013).

Further, in this work, it was notably established that MNEs show a preference to avoid competition between internal candidates by 'preparing' one person in advance, in most likelihood in order to avoid disruption and ensure the continuation of agreement and coordination within the firm, with both of these aspects recognised as influencing performance; the findings further recognise that DEs, in contrast, show a preference for external appointments for executive succession, which could ultimately facilitate the inclusion of innovative approaches and ideas into the system (Mohamed et al., 2013). When contrasted alongside domestic enterprises, it has been found that MNEs place much emphasis on sound individual technical skills for the purpose of promotion; this highlights their need to ensure the presence of technically knowledgeable and competent individuals in their senior roles. This is most likely owing to global organisational pressure, with the view that those individuals with a good degree of technical skills, especially in the manufacturing arena, are recognised as being better positioned to satisfy a job role specification than those without such abilities (Mohamed et al., 2013). One consideration that was not outlined for testing as an aim but which is nonetheless highlighted as requiring attention is that of the topical interest in 'talent management' across firms (Inskeep and Hall, 2008; Vaiman and Vance, 2008). In the present work, three fundamental aspects of talent management have undergone analysis, which further encompass additional aspects, including leadership development, replacement planning and mentoring. These areas, which are notably considered in the strategic HRM literature, are centred on achieving employee engagement with the aim of ultimately securing employee retention; these may prove to be critical considerations when it comes to achieving a competitive edge in the organisation's field (Becker et al., 2001; Mohamed et al., 2013). The findings garnered in the work presented in this chapter emphasise that there is a greater degree of strategy amongst MNEs compared with DEs when it comes to recruitment, training, and retention. Importantly, their absolute and apparent emphasis on such considerations could potentially be taken to infer effective talent management with the aim of ensuring they remain with the firm.

Implications

The current chapter acknowledges the advantages to be garnered through efficient and effective policies and practices in the arena of recruitment and selection, as implemented by firms when seeking to identify the most appropriate and fitting staff for their roles; these are pivotal to achieving organisational success (Mohamed et al., 2013). Should this practice be inappropriately adopted, HRM outcomes may not be desirable, with staff potentially seen to be lacking in motivation and morale, which is ultimately a situation that could incur additional costs for the business. Moreover, throughout the final phase of recruitment and selection, there is a need for HR directors to take into account the potential of candidates, with attention directed towards which attitudes, characteristics, qualifications and work-related values would be the most appropriate fit in line with the requirements of the offered positions, in addition to those that may be well aligned with the culture and requirements of the firm. This may effectively ensure that the tasks completed are done so as expected. The results garnered through the completion of the present study emphasise that, in the Brunei context, MNEs demonstrate a lesser tendency for staff turnover when compared with DEs functioning in the same context, with MNEs recognised as adopting more stringent and effective HR practices than those implemented by DEs. Such practices might include better training systems, more precisely outlined recruitment and selection approaches, and a larger number of internal career opportunities. In line with this, firms are therefore well positioned to ensure staff turnover rates are minimised at the onset of an individual's career; this can be achieved by ensuring the individual hired presents a valuable and close fit with the needs and requirements of the organisation and the role being filled. Similarly, extensive formal training also has the potential to achieve low figures in the number of staff leaving the organisation on an annual basis. Moreover, firms that promote and hire on an internal basis and actively prepare their staff for higher positions could achieve improvements in their employee turnover rates.

In conclusion, the empirical work presented in his chapter has emphasised a gap in the literature in the field of HR practices adopted by MNEs and DEs, with particular focus on the gap to be seen in relation to small, non-developed economies. Notably, there is the possibility that variations in HR practices could stem from national culture differences, the national view of HR in a particular country, which can notably involve some degree of historical competence, external firm factors, including government institution-presented regulations, internal firm factors, including ownership type and organisation size, and the role adopted by HR and the progression of such (Sparrow and Hiltrop, 1994; Shah et al., 2018; Zhu and Warner, 2019). Two of the hypotheses presented in this work have achieved validation, which provides a contrary and conflicting perspective when considering the value of HR amongst MNEs and DEs, with DEs' HR systems continuing to be recognised as lacking when compared with those adopted by MNEs. As has been shown by the contrasts completed in this work in regard to recruitment and selection, internal career opportunities, and training in MNEs and DEs, there is a very apparent distinction to be witnessed when reviewing the practices implemented by the two different types of organisation. Other works carried out in this arena that have provided contrasts in relation to HR practices applied by domestic and multinational organisations have, similarly, arrived at mixed findings, with the results garnered seeming to depend on the focus of the work, in addition to the context examined. Those works that have examined labour relations have shown a tendency to achieve both divergent and convergent results (see, for example, Ayentimi et al., 2018). Those works carried out in newly emerging or developed countries have further established divergent findings. Nonetheless, this chapter presents results that do not need to be viewed as an instance of 'reverse diffusion', to cite the work of Hayden and Edwards (2001), in which MNEs view their home systems as lacking when compared with the standards of the host country and as being difficult if not impossible to effectively transfer to their corresponding subsidiaries.

References

Appelbaum, E. and Batt, R. (1994). *The New American Workplace: Transforming Work Systems in the United States*, New York: ILR Press.

Ayentimi, D. T., Burgess, J. and Brown, K. (2018). HRM practices of MNEs and domestic firms in Ghana: Divergence or convergence? *Personnel Review*, 47, 1, 2–21.

Bao, C. and Analoui, F. (2011). An exploration of the impact of strategic international human resource management on firm performance: The case of foreign MNCs in China. *International Journal of Management and Information Systems*, 15, 4, 31–40.

Baron, J. (1988). The employment relation as a social relation. *Journal of Japanese and International Economies*, 2, 492–525.

Becker, B. E., Huselid, M. A., Huselid, M. A., & Ulrich, D. (2001). *The HR scorecard: Linking people, strategy, and performance*. Harvard Business Press.

Boxall, P., Purcell, J. and Wright, P. (2007). *The Oxford Handbook of Human Resource Management*, New York: Oxford University Press.

Budhwar, P. and Khatri, N. (2001). HRM in context: Applicability of HRM models in India. *International Journal of Cross Cultural Management*, 1, 3, 333–56.

Coff, R. W. (1997). Human assets and management dilemmas: Coping with hazards on the road to resource-based theory. *Academy of Management Review*, 22, 2, 374–402.

Cully, M. (1999). *Britain at Work: As Depicted by the 1998 Workplace Employee Relations Survey*, London: Routledge.

Darwish, T., Mohamed, A. F., Wood, G., Singh, S. and Fleming, J. (2017). Can HRM alleviate the negative effects of the resource curse on Firms? Evidence from Brunei. *Personnel Review*, 46, 8, 1931–1947.

Darwish, T., Singh, S. and Wood, G. (2016). The impact of human resource practices on actual and perceived organizational performance in a Middle-Eastern emerging market. *Human Resource Management*, 55, 2, 261–281.

De Guzman, G. M., Neelankavil, J. P. and Sengupta, K. (2011). Human resource roles: Ideal versus practiced: A cross-country comparison among organisations in Asia. *International Journal of Human Resource Management*, 22, 13, 2665–2682.

Dowling, P. J. and Schuler, R. S. (1990). *International Dimensions of Human Resource Management*, Boston, MA: PWS-Kent.

Dowling, P. J., Schuler, R. S. and Welch, D. (1999). *International Human Resource Management: Managing People in a Multinational Context*, Cincinnati, OH: South-Western College Publishing.

Guest, D. and Hoque, K. (1996). National ownership and HR practices in UK greenfield sites. *Human Resource Management Journal*, 6, 4, 50–74.

Haak-Saheem, W. and Brewster, C. (2017). "Hidden' expatriates: International mobility in the United Arab Emirates as a challenge to current understanding of expatriation. *Human Resource Management Journal*, 27, 3, 423–439.

Haak-Saheem, W., Festing, M. and Darwish, T. (2016). International Human Resource Management in the Arab Gulf States: An institutional perspective. *The International Journal of Human Resource Management*, 28, 18, 2684–2712.

Harel, G. H. and Tzafrir, S. S. (1999). The effect of human resource management practices on the perceptions of organizational and market performance of the firm. *Human Resource Management*, 3, 38, 185–200.

Harzing, A. W. and Sorge, A. (2003). The relative impact of country of origin and universal contingencies in internationalization strategies and corporate control in multination enterprises: Worldwide and European perspectives. *Organization Studies*, 24, 187–214.

Hayden, A. and Edwards, T. (2001). The erosion of the country of origin effect: A case study of a Swedish multinational company. *Industrial Relations*, 56, 116–140.

Hendry, C. (1994). *Human Resource Strategies for International Growth*, London: Routledge.

Hofstede, G. (1998). Think locally, act globally: Cultural constraints in personnel management. *Management International Review*, 38, 7–26.

Hoque, K. (1999). Human resource management and performance in the UK hotel industry. *British Journal of Industrial Relations*, 37, 3, 419–443.

Hsu, Y. and Leat, M. (2000). A study of HRM and recruitment and selection policies and practices in Taiwan. *International Journal of Human Resource Management*, 11, 2, 413–435.

Huang, T. (2000). Human resource management practices at subsidiaries of multinational corporations and local firms in Taiwan. *International Journal of Selection and Assessment*, 8, 1, 22–28.

Huselid, M. (1995). The impact of human resource management practices on turnover, productivity, and corporate financial performance. *Academy of Management Journal*, 38, 3, 635–670.

Inskeep, A. and Hall, B. (2008). Rewards and recognition concepts that support talent and knowledge management initiatives. In Vaiman, V. and Vance, C. M. (Eds.), *Smart Talent Management* (pp. 161–175). Cheltenham: Edward Elgar.

Jaw, B. S., Wang, C. Y. P. and Chen, Y. H. (2006). Knowledge flows and performance of multinational subsidiaries: The perspective of human capital. *International Journal of Human Resource Management*, 17, 2, 225–244.

Joseph, K. E. and Dai, C. (2009). HRM practices and organizational performance: An empirical analysis. *International Journal of Business and Management*, 4, 8, 117–127.

Lynch, L. M. and Black, S. E. (1995). Beyond the incidence of training; Evidence from a national employer survey. NBER Working Paper 5231, National Bureau of Economic Research, New York, NY.

Maertz, C. P. and Campion, M. A. (1998). 25 years of voluntary turnover research: A review and critique. In Cooper, C. L. and Robertson, I. T. (Eds.), *International Review of Industrial and Organizational Psychology*, vol. 13 (pp. 49–81). Chichester: Wiley.

Magner, N., Welker, R. B. and Johnson, G. G. (1996). The interactive effects of participation and outcome favourability on turnover intentions and evaluations of supervisors. *Journal of Occupational and Organizational Psychology*, 69, 2, 135–143.

Matlay, H. (1997). The paradox of training in the small business sector of the British economy. *Journal of Vocational Education and Training*, 49, 4, 573–88.

McGaughey, S. L. and De Cieri, H. (1999). Reassessment of convergence and divergence dynamics: Implications for international HRM. *International Journal of Human Resource Management*, 10, 2, 235–250.

Milgrom, P. (1988). Employment contracts, influence activities, and efficient organization design. *Journal of Political Economy*, 96, 42–60.

Miller, J. S., Hom, P. W. and Gomez-Mejia, L. R. (2001). The high cost of low wages: Does Maquiladora compensation reduce turnover? *Journal of International Business Studies*, 32, 3, 585–595.

Mohamed, F., Singh, S., Irani, Z. and Darwish, T. (2013). An analysis of recruitment, training and retention practices in domestic and multinational enterprises in the country of Brunei Darussalam. *International Journal of Human Resource Management*, 24, 10, 2054–2081.

Myloni, B., Harzing, A. K. and Mirza, H. (2004). Human resource management in Greece: Have the colours of culture faded away? *International Journal of Cross Cultural Management*, 4, 1, 59–76.

Noe, R. A., Hollenbeck, J. R., Gerhart, B., and Wright, P. M. (2006). *Human Resources Management: Gaining a Competitive Advantage*, New York: Mc-Graw-Hill.

Osman-Gani, A. M., and Jacobs, R. L. (2005). Technological change and human resource development practices in Asia: A study of Singapore-based companies. *International Journal of Training and Development*, 9, 4, 271–280.

Pfeffer, J. (1994). *Competitive Advantage through People*, Boston, MA: Harvard Business School Press.

Reiche, B. S. (2008). The configuration of employee retention practices in multinational corporations' foreign subsidiaries. *International Business Review*, 17, 676–687.

Rowley, C. and Benson, J. (2002). Convergence and divergence in Asian HRM. *California Management Review*, 44, 2, 90–109.

Rugman, A. M. and Collinson. S. (2009). *International Business*. 4th ed. London: FT Prentice Hall.

Scullion, H. (1995). International human resource management. In Storey, J. (Ed.), *Human Resource Management: A Critical Text* (pp. 352–382). London: Routledge.

Shah, S., Anwar, J. and Hasnu, S. (2018). Does location matter in determining firms' performance? A comparative analysis of domestic and multinational companies. *Journal of Asia Business Studies*, 12, 3, 253–272.

Shaw, J. D., Delery, J. E., Jenkins, G. D. and Gupta, N. (1998). An organization-level analysis of voluntary and involuntary turnover. *Academy of Management Journal*, 41, 5, 511–525.

Shen, J. and Darby, R. (2006). Training and management development in Chinese multinational enterprises. *Employee Relations*, 28, 4, 342–362.

Shen, J. and Edwards, V. (2004). Recruitment and selection in Chinese MNEs. *International Journal of Human Resource Management*, 15, 814–835.

Singh, S., Darwish, T., Wood, G. and Mohamed. A. F. (2017). Institutions, complementarity, human resource management and performance in a South-East Asian Petrostate: The case of Brunei. *The International Journal of Human Resource Management*, 28, 18, 2538–2569.

Singh, S., Wood, G., Darwish, T., Fleming, J. and Mohammed, A. F. (2019). Human resource management in multinational and domestic enterprises:

A comparative institutional analysis in Southeast Asia. *Thunderbird International Business Review*, 61, 229–241.

Sparrow, P. R. and Hiltrop, J. M. (1994). *European Human Resource Management in Transition*, London: Prentice Hall.

Sparrow, P. R., Schuler, R. S. and Jackson, S. E. (1994). Convergence or divergence: Human resource practices and policies for competitive advantage worldwide. *International Journal of Human Resource Management*, 5, 2, 267–300.

Szamosi, L. T., Duxbury, L. and Higgins, C. (2004). Toward an understanding of people management issues in SMEs: A South-Eastern European perspective. *Education and Training*, 46, 8, 444–465.

Tan, H. (2001). Do training levies work? Malaysia's HRDF and its effects on training and firm-level productivity, Working Paper, World Bank, Washington, DC.

Vaiman, V. and Vance, C. M. (2008). *Smart Talent Management*. Cheltenham: Edward Elgar.

Van Smoorenburg, M. S. M. and Van der Velden, R. K. W. (2000). The training of school leavers: Complementarity or substitution? *Economics of Education Review*, 19, 2, 207–217.

Verburg, R. M. (1998). *Human Resource Management: Optimale HRM-praktijken en Con. guraties*, Dissertation. Amsterdam: Vrije Universiteit.

Von Glinow, M. A., Huo, Y. and Lowe, P. K. (1999). Leadership across the Pacific Ocean: A transactional comparison. *International Business Review*, 8, 1–15.

Way, S. (2002). High performance work systems and intermediate indicators of firm performance within the US small business sector. *Journal of Management*, 28, 765–785.

Winterton, J. (2007). Training, development and competence. In Boxall, P., Purcell, J. and Wright, P. (Eds.), *The Oxford Handbook of Human Resource Management* (pp. 324–343). Oxford: Oxford University Press.

Wright, P., Szeto, W. F. and Cheng, L. T. W. (2002). Guanxi and professional conduct in China: A management development perspective. *International Journal of Human Resource Management*, 13, 1, 156–182.

Zheng, C., Hyland, P. and Soosay, C. (2007). Training practices of multinational companies in Asia. *Journal of European Industrial Training*, 31, 6, 472–494.

Zheng, C., Morrison, M. and O'Neill, G. (2006). An empirical study of high performance HR practices in Chinese SMEs. *International Journal of Human Resource Management*, 17, 10, 1772–1803.

Zhu, C. and Warner, M. (2019). The emergence of human resource management in China: Convergence, divergence and contextualization. *Human Resource Management Review*, 29, 1, 87–97.

9 Performance Appraisals, Incentives, and Reward Practices in Domestic Vs Multinational Enterprises

Satwinder Singh, Pengiran Muda Abdul Fattaah, and Tamer K Darwish

Introduction

One critical advance in the arena of International Business (IB) throughout the past twenty years has been recognised in development of MNEs, which are currently viewed as being one of the key factors driving globalisation (Singh et al., 2013). The worldwide increase in these entities has created a foundation upon which the international human resource management (IHRM) studies which examine HRM and its individual components – incentives, recruitment, rewards, training, etc. – can be developed (Ghoshal & Bartlett, 1990; Pucik, 1997; Haak-Saheem et al., 2016), Studies completed across MNEs are commonly focused on developing insight into the way in which MNEs implement make use of expatriates in subsidiaries, and the ways in which employees are managed, selected and trained (Dowling & Welch, 2004; Haak-Saheem & Brewster, 2017); these are commonly vulnerable to host nations' cultural traits (Gooderham & Brewster, 2003), as well as to the existence of the social context intrinsic within the economic and social institutions of host countries (Morishima, 1995; Singh et al., 2013), Literature review, as provided below, highlights that, despite various works having been carried out on MNE affiliates' HRM practices, it remains that only limited amount of work in this direction has been carried out as comparative studies amongst MNE affiliates in emerging host countries. There is none so far in the context of Brunei Darussalam (Mohamed et al., 2013; Singh et al., 2013). This chapter provides an insight into this previously unexplored area in the literature, achieved through the completion of a comparative analysis of three major HR practices, namely performance appraisals (referred to as PAs), incentives and rewards in MNE affiliates and DEs operating in this country.

This chapter has following sections: it first provides an overview of the literature in the field of HR practices, following which we list the testable hypotheses; and discuss the results and finally, conclusions are then drawn followed by discussion.

Performance Appraisals

Performance Appraisals (PAs) are tools to assess the performance of workforce through objective, rational and systematic means. The process of appraisals embraces various elements of HR practices–conflict resolution, communication, employee reactions, equity and fairness, feedback, trust, and acceptance (Lawler, 2003; Chiang & Birtch, 2010; Darwish et al., 2016). Incorporated within work motivation theory, an appraisal system is deemed necessary to facilitate identification of the differences between performing employees so as to enable rewards to be efficiently and equally distributed, in addition to effectively communicating business needs and requirements; such a process aids in employee retention as well as in attracting new talent to the company (Singh et al., 2013). Several HR scholars have emphasised the potential benefits of appraisals following on from the administration, development, documentation and evaluation of staff; utilising such a method as a tool for communication, coaching, and expression (Hempel, 2001; Milliman et al., 2002). Performance Appraisals have also been utilised in an effort to achieve a more top–down controlling performance management style alongside administrative decisions, including the decision of compensation and promotion in line with the performance criteria evaluated throughout the appraisal process (Gomez-Mejia et al., 2004). Furthermore, appraisals have been carried out through a new approach of communicating development requirements, emphasising the gaps in the performance of an employee, and further explaining the expectations of the business, as well as role objectives, whilst also outlining future training and development designs (DeNisi & Pritchard, 2006).

A wealth of empirical work has been completed in regard to HR practices when taking into account cross-national and intercultural instances; nonetheless, the PA approach has not been examined in-depth throughout the course of such efforts (Milliman et al., 2002; Chiang & Birtch, 2010). Performance Appraisals have been investigated in the instance of cross-natural works (Aycan, 2000; Milliman et al., 2002), whereas other works have been more inclined to place emphasis on the more exceptional elements of appraisal, and are fundamental US-geared (Amba-Rao et al., 2000; Entrekin & Chung, 2001; Groeschl, 2003).

Incentives and Rewards

Rewards, as a concept, has been more officially outlined as something given to a receiver and recognised as valuable and appreciated as a result of work; this may be financial, as such as through the provision of an increase in wage or otherwise as a bonus, as highlighted in the work by Chiang and Birtch (2007), or alternatively could be non-financial, as in the case of cognitive or effective rewards (Elizur et al., 1991; Darwish et al., 2016). In essence, rewards and incentives are seen to be a key approach followed by organisations in achieving the best outcomes and behaviours from employees, with this particular approach seen to be one of the most efficient HR practices when striving to both manage and maintain sound and consistent levels of performance across staff (Huselid, 1995; Delery & Doty, 1996; Darwish et al., 2013).

It is noteworthy to highlight that, across some businesses, the reward system has demonstrated much change from providing staff with compensation in line with non-performance factors, including in the case of years' experience and seniority, for example, with compensation in line with firm contribution recognised as now more commonly implemented in firms (Lawler, 2000; Singh et al., 2013), with the latter meaning entitlement mentality is reduced, whilst also achieving an increase in employee ability and performance through performance, as well as the ability to offer skills-based rewards (Heneman et al., 2000). Staff achieving the required performance-related levels are provided with a reward in line with their efforts, which therefore highlights a clear link between performance and pay, recognised as a key driving motivational factor (Lawler & Jenkins, 1992; Darwish et al., 2016). Skill-based reward and incentive initiatives may further be recognised as a motivator for staff to develop and broaden their skillset and knowledge base; this could subsequently enhance the overall intellectual capital of the firm (Beatty et al., 2003; Singh et al., 2017). Those incentives and rewards that are job-based are seen to have stemmed from equity theory, which seeks to attain and ensure consistency and fairness across the firm, with rewards afforded in line with job worth (Greenberg, 1990).

It has been stated that external equity drivers, including labour market conditions and comparable industry wage levels, for example, need to be considered in line with the view that employee satisfaction through suitable reward and incentive systems may help to improve fairness, both internally and externally (Chiang & Birtch, 2007). As has been established through the completion of more recent works, the orientation of rewards and incentives has been redirected to be more strategic, with the suggestion made that, if implemented in the right way, a well-designed system could facilitate organisations in achieving and maintaining a business edge (Delery & Doty, 1996; Boxall & Purcell, 2003; Darwish et al., 2016; Singh et al., 2019).

The literature available in the field of incentives and rewards has predominantly centred on individual factors, including benefits in comparison with money – either in terms of financial rewards or non-financial, or in line with particular types of staff, as in the case of different incentives or rewards being provided to executives or expatriates (Hempel, 1998; Fay & Thompson, 2001; Lowe et al., 2002; Haak-Saheem & Brewster, 2017). Prior studies have further centred on manager viewpoints in relation to reward and incentive preferences as held by staff as opposed to actual staff viewpoints (Bigoness & Blakely, 1996; Oliver & Cravens, 1999). A comprehensive examination into rewards and incentives thus far appears to have been without much attention (Lowe et al., 2002; Singh et al., 2013).

Literature Gaps and Necessary Comparisons

Owing to globalisation, firms are now competing with one another on a worldwide scale as opposed to simply directing their attention to regional markets, as has been highlighted by scholars (Bartlett & Ghoshal, 1998; Singh et al., 2013). There is a need to recognise, however, that it is posited by some that most MNEs should and do actively implement strategies centred on strategic competitiveness, either on a local or regional basis (Rugman, 2003). In this vein, Bartlett and Ghoshal (1998) highlight the value of national responsiveness, which considers the fact that, from one market to the next, customer preferences will change; therefore, it would be beneficial to ensure products and services are adapted in line with local requirements; as a result, national responsiveness would further incorporate cultural differences, with such variations recognised across behaviours, communication, expectations and negotiation, all of which are important when it comes to implementing an international strategy (Singh et al., 2013). Regardless, however, there is a need for MNEs to recognise the value of HRM across the worldwide domain (Sparrow & Brewster, 2006; Haak-Saheem et al., 2016). Such a consideration needs to be taken into account owing to the fact that scholars and academics have previously established different concepts, including best practices and benchmarking, as fundamental requirements for a HR system; in contrast, however, other professionals have established degrees of convergence from one country to the next, in addition to entirely contrasting methods depending on environment (Brewster et al., 2008; Ayentimi et al., 2018; Singh et al., 2019). In essence, it is also imperative that any shift from older or less developed HR policies and practices is accepted, with the same in reverse also accepted (Singh et al., 2013). Accordingly, it is important that the ways in which HRM systems adapt in line with varying settings are also understood. In this regard, this chapter provides further insight through examining the PA, rewards, and incentives process in DEs and MNEs in an effort to establish whether or not behavioural differences can be identified across the two types of firm.

HR Practices and Culture

The ever-increasing value assigned to across-border operation has meant that culture effect has been viewed as more important; this has come to be the case with appraisals as well (Singh et al., 2013). Academics in the field have come to identify and recognise the association between culture and HR practices, with appraisals recognised as more inclined to be aligned with a particular society's belief, norms and values (Sparrow et al., 1994; Darwish et al., 2016; Haak-Saheem et al., 2016). Importantly, differences in culture are also seen to adopt a key role in the completion of PAs, in addition to the way in which management and employees view such practice (Singh et al., 2013). As an example, in Western societies, the frank and open approach is implemented and is commonplace; however, this is not always the case in other contexts, including in Asia, for example, where such an approach would be viewed as leading to 'losing face' (Easterby-Smith et al., 1995).

It should be recognised that other works have also recognised associations between rewards and incentives, and cultural influence, with academics in this regard recognising various HR practices as going hand-in-hand with varying levels of sensitivity to culture: for example, HR planning, as a 'hard' practice is seen to be more sensitive to cultural values; 'soft' practices, on the other hand, are viewed as being linked with the motivational considerations of staff (Easterby-Smith et al., 1995; Rowley & Benson, 2002; Darwish et al., 2016). Taking into account cultural viewpoints when implementing incentives and rewards is further seen to be a pressing consideration, with the exploration of various contexts that are able to aid in theory development. As an example, motivation theory, which is seen to provide clear support for rewards and incentives, is seen to stem from the West; this causes bias to be present, in addition to more Westernised perspectives pertaining to employee requirements (Boyacigiller & Adler, 1991; Singh et al., 2013).

It is apparent there has been inadequate focus directed towards the completion of a comparative analysis of HRM practices between indigenous and foreign-owned organisations. With HRM practices implemented in MNE subsidiaries the common focus for comparisons, has been carried out in developed regions (Guest & Hoque, 1996; Muller, 1998; Geary & Roche, 2001). It is important to highlight that prior works that have provided a contrast between HR practices in MNEs and DEs have secured varied findings depending on the research focus, in addition to the context of the work (Ayentimi et al., 2018; Shah et al., 2018; Zhu and Warner, 2019). As an example, those researches reviewing labour relations have arrived at 'convergent' proposition findings. Furthermore, works centred on non-industrialised regions have identified 'divergent' proposition findings (Yuen & Kee, 1993; Chen et al., 2005); though convergence was recognised in some cases in these studies (see, for example, Ayentimi et al. 2018).

Hypotheses

One of the most commonly held behaviours and underpinnings identifiable in IB literature (surveys worthy of review may be reviewed in the works of Boxall et al. (2007) and Rugman (2009)), as touched upon above, is that, owing to the fact that MNEs operate on a worldwide basis, these deal with a more rigid and competitive environments than DEs (Haak-saheem et al., 2016). In an effort to satisfy the more threatening of competition and the continuous risk posed by new organisations, the point is argued that MNEs are consistently seeking to improve the standards of their operations in such a way so as to improve their competitive edge and accordingly remain abreast of competitors; accordingly, when considering the issue of core importance, as in the case of HRM, a more strategic and structured approach is implemented by MNEs, which may be argued as being more stringent and thorough than those adopted by DEs (Singh et al., 2013; Haak-Saheem et al., 2016). One rationale for this could be that, whilst DEs are susceptible to influence stemming from local beliefs, norms and values, the effects of such traits on MNEs would be minimal; however, it would not be possible for them to be entirely disregarded if they are to work well in host regions (Mohamed et al., 2013; Singh et al., 2013; Shah et al., 2018; Zhu and Warner, 2019). In line with this, as well as in consideration to the literature discussed above, following hypotheses are proposed.

H1: No significant difference can be identified between DEs and MNEs in terms of the frequency with which PAs are carried out, who completes the PAs, and the period of time within which PA feedback is provided to staff.

H2: The PA process will be better accepted by MNEs' HR directors and employees than in the case of DEs.

H3: A number of market principles and ethos are adopted by MNEs when it comes to describing the rewards and incentives initiative to staff, with such an approach less commonly identifiable in DEs.

H4: In relation to organisation's size and age, when contrasted alongside DEs, larger, longer-established MNEs' staff and management would be seen to be more receptive to market-based rewards and incentives than those MNEs that are smaller and younger in age.

As can be seen from the first hypothesis, which centre on the fundamentals of completing PAs, it is not expected that, when comparing DEs to MNEs, that there will be any difference. The second and third hypotheses emphasise that, in consideration to their global positioning, PAs, rewards and incentives may be better developed and more thoroughly structured in the case of MNEs than in DEs. The fourth and final hypothesis examines the overall validity of control variables, where longer established and bigger firms are predicted as being more open to market-based PA principles, rewards and incentives when compared with smaller, more recently established organisations. For the work presented in this chapter, data are collected from a primary survey, across DEs' and MNEs' HR Directors in the context of Brunei Darussalam. 151 replies were obtained (88 were from DEs and 63 were from MNEs). The latter has greatly helped in achieving the comparative nature of this work (for more details in relation to measurement, data, and analysis, see Singh et al. 2013).

Discussion and Conclusions

It has been established throughout the work presented in this chapter that, when it comes to motivating staff to direct optimal levels of effort for the benefit of the organisation, appraisals, incentives and rewards, and HR practices can be pivotal (Singh et al., 2103; Darwish et al., 2016). Accordingly, the focus of this work has been centred on garnering insight into how such practices can be provided, described, and monitored in DEs in comparison to MNEs, in addition to establishing the similarity or difference in nature. Following on from the completion of the literature review, we proposed that, in consideration to the wide-ranging perspective and international competitive environment in which these firms function, HR practices would be seen to be more structurally implemented in MNEs, adhering to more market-based principles, when compared with DEs, whose staff would be found to be more open to the adoption of such practices.

As emphasised by Singh et al. (2013), primary data gathered from both domestic and foreign organisations operating in Brunei highlight valuable findings, which emphasise that PAs are more commonly adopted in MNEs than in DEs, and that the former's feedback is also much quicker; the latter went against the estimations of the researchers, as detailed in the first hypothesis; it was considered that there would not be any identifiable difference when reviewing this issue in the case of MNEs and DEs. Notably, however, the second hypothesis has been confirmed through the results, with MNEs' staff and HR directors found to be more receptive to PA in the case of DEs. A more in-depth analysis provided further validation for the third hypothesis, which postulated that, in MNEs, incentives and rewards would adhere to market principles and ethos more so than DEs. Nonetheless, an in-depth examination into the sample with regard to organisations' age and size provided only partial support for the last hypothesis, which suggested that larger and longer established MNEs' employees and HR directors would be open and responsive to PAs than those hired by Des; the findings have emphasised that, generally speaking, more recently established organisations are more likely to adhere to market principles in terms of providing staff with explanations as to their rewards and incentives. Those organisations that have been longer established, in contrast, suggest psychological and social advantages to working with such firms.

When drawing a comparison between DEs and MNEs, the former does not appear to have any key implementation when it comes to incentives and rewards, which may be recognised as potentially owing to the nature of globalisation as a whole. When it comes to DEs' and MNEs' PA process and the acceptance of such, it is primarily imperative to develop insight into the culture intrinsic as part of a host country. Research investing the placement of Brunei, in line with the dimensions of culture presented by Hofstede, have been carried out and subsequently found to highlight very apparent and clear attributes when compared alongside their neighbours, as in the cases of Malaysia and Indonesia, in addition to other regions in South-East Asia (Singh et al., 2013; Darwish et al., 2017). As an example, it is noted in the work of Blunt (1989) that, despite there being a number of comparable aspects between Brunei and other South-East Asian countries, including medium masculinity, high-power–distance nation, and low individualism, for example, it remains that strong uncertainty avoidance is identifiable amongst Brunei firms. This has been pinpointed in the work of Hofstede (1983), who states that the country's characteristics show development and modernisation, with much change facing those societies with inflexible religious paths and young generations – all of which may be recognised as the case in the Brunei context.

Such cultural qualities have been recognised as influencing HR practices, as applied in an organisation (Darwish et al., 2016). As an example, the high power–distance apparent in Brunei may provide some explanation as to why in contrast with their domestic firms, with MNE staff and management more open to and accepting of personal appraisals and the process of such (Singh et al., 2019). Different to DEs, MNEs are more likely to implement a decentralised approach to decision-making, placing emphasis on the value of mutual communication from regions known to have a lower power–distance ratio (Hofstede, 2001). Owing to the fact that the management style fosters and advances low power–distance cultures, trust is recognised as being established and further developed between a supervisor and staff, particularly when they work together or communicate in relation to job-associated performance considerations (Rousseau et al., 1998). Other works carried out in this area (e.g., Shane, 1993; Doney et al., 1998; Singh et al., 2019) have come to recognise that control and trust criteria are both affected and shaped by the power–distance ratio, and are in essence in contrast. The findings garnered in this chapter further highlight such works' conclusions, with MNEs seen to demonstrate a lower power–distance ratio recognised as well-positioned to create and further enhance levels of trust when completing PAs owing to their more instruction-centred and facilitating role (Singh et al., 2013). In contrast, however, in the case of high power–distance organisations, as in the case of DEs operating in Brunei and other similar regions, PAs may be applied as a means of achieving control, as has been highlighted in the studies by Entrekin and Chung (2001) and Chiang and Birtch (2007). Culture's impact further extends to the overall acceptance of subordinate feedback, with the findings garnered in this chapter suggesting that, in the context of Brunei, a greater degree of feedback opposition may be witnessed; this can be owing to PA's overriding objective and implementation; in such an instance, MNEs make use of PAs from an educational standpoint, whilst DEs, on the other hand, make use of this tool in a judicial role (Singh et al., 2013). Owing to the fact that DEs are known to have a greater power–distance ratio, they similarly have a more hierarchical structure with PAs carried out in mind of validating and further reinforcing promotion and compensation decisions (Singh et al., 2013). However, in such cases, it is not possible for opposing views to be articulated due to loyalty and the respect for authority, meaning subordinates feel the need to accept whatever assessments and choices are presented by their management (Milliman et al., 1998). As has been noted earlier, this goes against the attributes of low power–distance firms that adopt decentralised decision-making and place importance on two-way communication, adopting the standpoint that improved performance will be achieved when staff understand and are aligned with organisation expectations (Hofstede, 2001; Singh et al., 2013). Involvement in and ownership of PA outcomes can also further improve performance, with staff communicating their opinions and interacting with supervisors; this provides further clarification of job expectations (Chiang & Birch, 2010).

When reviewing the rewards and incentives commonly implemented across firms in Brunei, the survey data findings highlight DEs as being more inclined to consider industry standards when devising and implementing their own rewards, as in the case of pay, for example; this is seen to be most likely as a result of enhanced competition in the country as a result of the actions implemented by neighbouring countries, in addition to the inclination of the domestic government to observe the approaches applied by Singapore in consideration to the close nature of their relationship (Singh et al., 2013). Without question, it is apparent that a key role is adopted by culture in terms of the nature of rewards of preference across a firm's staff; in the empirical work presented in this chapter, the findings may be seen to provide support for the firm's cultural learnings, in addition to the culture of the host country overall (Singh et al., 2013).

In conclusion, this chapter emphasises a number of critical and valuable differences identifiable at the centre of HR appraisal and rewards system practices in the case of both DEs and foreign organisations. The former of these may also present managerial lessons as established from the practices implemented by the latter – particularly if the foreign firms' financial results are seen to be greater. The findings may be of value to other host regions recognised as having comparable attributes when compared to Brunei, in addition to those MNEs aiming to enter into and operate in the region; it is considered that such lines could be further expanded on in future academic works, such as through examining the factors underpinning the various differences identifiable in HR practices (Singh et al., 2013).

References

Amba-Rao, S.C., Petrick, J.A., Gupta, J.N.D., & Von der Embse, T.J. (2000). Comparative performance appraisal practices and management values among foreign and domestic firms in India. *The International Journal of Human Resource Management*, 11, 66–89.

Aycan, Z. (2000). Cross-cultural industrial and organisational psychology: Contributions, past developments and future directions. *The International Journal of Human Resource Management*, 31, 110–128.

Ayentimi, D.T., Burgess, J., & Brown, K. (2018). HRM practices of MNEs and domestic firms in Ghana: divergence or convergence? *Personnel Review*, 47, 1, 2–21.

Bartlett, C.A., & Ghoshal, S. (1998). *Managing Across Borders: The Transnational Solution* (2nd ed.). Boston, MA: Harvard Business School Press.

Beatty, R.W., Huselid, M.A., Schneier, C.E., & New, H.R. (2003). Metrics: Scoring on the business scorecard. *Organizational Dynamics*, 32, 107–121.

Bigoness, W.J., & Blakely, G.L. (1996). A cross-national study of managerial values. *Journal of International Business Studies*, 27, 739–752.

Blunt, P. (1989). Cultural consequences for organization change in a Southeast Asian state: Brunei. *The Academy of Management Executive (1987–1989)*, 2, 235–240.

Boxall, P., & Purcell, J. (2003). *Strategy and Human Resource Management*. New York: Palgrave, Macmillan.

Boxall, P., Purcell, J., & Wright, P. (2007). *The Oxford Handbook of Human Resource Management*. Oxford: Oxford University Press.

Boyacigiller, N.A., & Adler, N.J. (1991). The parochial dinosaur: The organizational sciences in a global context. *Academy of Management Review*, 16, 262–290.

Brewster, C., Wood, G., & Brookes, M. (2008). Similarity, isomorphism and duality? Recent survey evidence on the HRM policies of MNCs. *British Journal of Management*, 19, 4, 320–342.

Chen, S.J., Lawler, J.J., & Bae, J. (2005). Convergence in human resource systems: A comparison of locally owned and MNC subsidiaries in Taiwan. *Human Resource Management*, 44, 237–256.

Chiang, F., & Birtch, T. (2007). The transferability of management practices: Examining crossnational differences in reward preferences. *Human Relations*, 60, 1293–1330.

Chiang, F., & Birtch, T. (2010). Appraising performance across borders: An empirical examination of the purposes and practices of performance appraisal in a multi-country context. *Journal of Management Studies*, 47, 1365–1393.

Darwish, T., Singh, S. & Mohamed, A.F. (2013). The role of strategic HR practices in organisational effectiveness: An investigation in the country of Jordan. *International Journal of Human Resource Management*, 24, 17, 3343–3362.

Darwish, T., Singh, S. & Wood, G. (2016). The impact of human resource practices on actual and perceived organizational performance in a Middle-Eastern emerging market. *Human Resource Management*, 55, 2, 261–281.

Darwish, T., Mohamed, A.F., Wood, G., Singh, S. & Fleming, J. (2017). Can HRM alleviate the negative effects of the resource curse on Firms? Evidence from Brunei. *Personnel Review*, 46, 8, 1931–1947.

Delery, J.E., & Doty, D.H. (1996). Modes of theorizing in strategic human resource management: Tests of universalistic, contingency and configurational performance prediction. *Academy of Management Journal*, 39, 802–835.

DeNisi, A.S., & Pritchard, R.D. (2006). Performance appraisal, performance management and improving individual performance: A motivational framework. *Management and Organisation Review*, 2, 253–277.

Doney, P.M., Cannon, J.P., & Mullen, M. (1998). Understanding the influence of national culture on the development of trust. *Academy of Management*, 23, 601–619.

Dowling, P.J., & Welch, D.E. (2004). *International Human Resource Management: Managing People in a Multinational Context* (4th ed.). London: Thomson.

Easterby-Smith, M., Mailna, D., & Yuan, D. (1995). How culture sensitive is HRM? A comparative analysis of practice in Chinese and UK companies. *The International Journal of Human Resource Management*, 6, 31–59.

Elizur, D., Borg, I., Hunt, R., & Beck, I.M. (1991). The structure of work values: A cross cultural comparison. *Journal of Organizational Behavior*, 12, 21–38.

Entrekin, L., & Chung, Y.W. (2001). Attitudes towards different sources of executive appraisal: A comparison of Hong Kong Chinese and American managers in Hong Kong. *The International Journal of Human Resource Management*, 12, 965–987.

Fay, C.H., & Thompson, M.A. (2001). Contextual determinants of reward systems' success: An exploratory study. *Human Resource Management*, 40, 213–226.

Ferner, A. (1997). Country of origin effects and HRM in multinational companies. *Human Resource Management Journal*, 7, 19–37.

Geary, J.F., & Roche, W.K. (2001). Multinationals and human resource practices in Ireland: A rejection of the "new conformance thesis. *The International Journal of Human Resource Management*, 12, 109–127.

Ghoshal, S., & Bartlett, C.A. (1990). The multinational corporation as an interorganizational network. *Academy of Management Review*, 15, 603–625.

Gomez-Mejia, L.R., Balkin, D.B., & Cardy, R.L. (2004). *Managing Human Resources*, Upper Saddle River, NJ: Prentice-Hall.

Gooderham, P.N., & Brewster, C. (2003). Convergence, stasis or divergence? Personnel Management in Europe. *Scandinavian Journal of Business Research*, 17, 6–18.

Greenberg, J. (1990). Organizational justice: Yesterday, today, and tomorrow. *Journal of Management*, 16, 399–432.

Groeschl, S. (2003). Cultural implications for the appraisal process. *Cross Cultural Management*, 10, 67–79.

Guest, D.E., & Hoque, K. (1996). National ownership and HR practices in UK Greenfield sites. *Human Resource Management Journal*, 6, 50–74.

Haak-Saheem, W., & Brewster, C. (2017). Hidden' expatriates: international mobility in the United Arab Emirates as a challenge to current understanding of expatriation. *Human Resource Management Journal*, 27, 3, 423–439.

Haak-Saheem, W., Festing, M., & Darwish, T. (2016). International human resource management in the Arab Gulf States: An institutional perspective. *The International Journal of Human Resource Management*, 28, 18, 2684–2712.

Hempel, P.S. (1998). Designing multinational benefits programs: The role of national culture. *Journal of World Business*, 33, 277–294.

Hempel, P.S. (2001). Differences between Chinese and Western managerial views of performance. *Personnel Review*, 30, 203–206.

Heneman, R.L., Ledford, G.E., & Gresham, M.T. (2000). The changing nature of work and its effects on compensation design and delivery. In *Compensation in Organizations: Current Research and Practice*, eds. S. Rynes & B. Gerhart, San Francisco, CA: Jossey-Bass, pp. 195–240.

Hofstede, G. (1983). Dimensions of national cultures in fifty countries and three regions. In *expiscations in cross cultural psychology*, eds. J.B. Deregowski, S. Dziuraweic, & R.C. Annis, The Netherlands: Swets and Zeitlinger, pp. 335–355.

Hofstede, G. (2001). *Culture's Consequences: Comparing Values, Behaviors, Institutions, and Organizations across Nations*. Thousand Oaks, CA: Sage.

Huselid, M. (1995). The impact of human resource management practices on turnover, productivity, and corporate financial performance. *Academy of Management Journal*, 38, 635–670.

Lawler, E.E. (2000). *Rewarding Excellence: Pay Strategies for the New Economy*. San Francisco, CA: Jossey-Bass.

Lawler, E.E. (2003). Reward practices and performance management system effectiveness. *Organizational Dynamics*, 32, 396–404.

Lawler, E.E., & Jenkins, G.D. (1992). Strategic reward systems. In *Handbook of Industrial and Organizational Psychology* (Vol. 2), eds. M. Dunnette & L. Hough, Palo Alto, CA: Consulting Psychologists Press, pp. 1009–1055.

Milliman, J., Nason, S., Gallagher, E., Huo, P., Von Glinow, M.A., & Lowe, K.B. (1998). The impact of national culture on human resource management practices: The case of performance appraisal. *Advances in International Comparative Management*, 12, 157–183.

Milliman, J., Nason, S., Zhu, C., & De Cieri, H. (2002). An exploratory assessment of the purposes of performance appraisals in North and Central America and the Pacific Rim. *Human Resource Management*, 41, 87–102.

Mohamed, F., Singh, S., Irani, Z., & Darwish, T. (2013). An analysis of recruitment, training, and retention practices in domestic and multinational enterprises in the country of Brunei Darussalam. *The International Journal of Human Resource Management*, 24, 2054–2081.

Morishima, M. (1995). Embedding HRM in a social context. *British Journal of Industrial Relations*, 33, 617–640.

Muller, M. (1998). Human resource and industrial relations practices of UK and US multinationals in Germany. *The International Journal of Human Resource Management*, 9, 732–749.

Oliver, E.G., & Cravens, K.S. (1999). Cultural influences on managerial choice: An empirical study of employee benefit plans in the United States. *Journal of International Business Studies*, 30, 745–762.

Pucik, V. (1997). Human Resources in the Future: An Obstacle or a Champion of Globalization? In *Tomorrow's HR management*, eds. D. Ulrich, M. Losey, & G. Lake, New York: Wiley, pp. 320–327.

Rousseau, D.M., Sitkin, S.B., Burt, R.S., & Camerer, C. (1998). Not so different after all: A cross-discipline view of trust. *Academy of Management Review*, 23, 393–404.

Rowley, C., & Benson, J. (2002). Convergence and divergence in Asian HRM. *California Management Review*, 44, 90–109.

Rugman, A. (2003). Regional strategy and the demise of globalization. *Journal of International Management*, 9, 409–417.

Rugman, A. (2009). *The Oxford Handbook of International Business*. Oxford: Oxford University Press.

Shah, S., Anwar, J., & Hasnu, S (2018). Does location matter in determining firms' performance? A comparative analysis of domestic and multinational companies. *Journal of Asia Business Studies*, 12, 3, 253–272.

Shane, S.A. (1993). The effects of cultural differences in perceptions of transaction costs on national differences in the preference for international joint ventures. *Asia Pacific Journal of Management*, 10, 57–69.

Singh, S., Darwish, T., Wood, G. & Mohamed. A.F. (2017). Institutions, complementarity, human resource management and performance in a South-East Asian Petrostate: The case of Brunei. *The International Journal of Human Resource Management*, 28, 18, 2538–2569.

Singh, S., Mohamed, F. & Darwish, T. (2013). A comparative study of performance appraisals, incentives and rewards practices in domestic and multinational enterprises in the country of Brunei Darussalam. *International Journal of Human Resource Management*, 24, 19, 3577–3598.

Singh, S., Wood, G., Darwish, T., Fleming, J. & Mohammed, A.F. (2019). Human resource management in multinational and domestic enterprises: A comparative institutional analysis in Southeast Asia. *Thunderbird International Business Review*, 61, 229–241.

Sparrow, P.R., & Brewster, C. (2006). Globalizing HRM: The Growing Revolution in Managing Employees Internationally. In *The Human Resources Revolution: Research and Practice*, eds. C. Cooper & R. Burke. London: Elsevier, 99–122.

Sparrow, P.R., Schuler, R.S., & Jackson, S.F. (1994). Convergence or divergence: Human resource practices and policies for competitive advantage worldwide. *The International Journal of Human Resource Management*, 5, 267–299.

Yuen, E.C., & Kee, H.T. (1993). Headquarters, host-culture and organizational influences on HRM policies and practices. *Management International Review*, 33, 361–383.

Zhu, C. & Warner, M. (2019). The emergence of human resource management in China: Convergence, divergence and contextualization. *Human Resource Management Review*, 29, 1, 87–97.

10 A Comparative Perspective on HRM in Brunei

Geoffrey Wood

Introduction

There has been a growing body of work on HRM in a wide cross section of emerging markets. There was initially a strong focus on cross-cultural approaches that sought to explain both the dominance of specific types of practice in emerging markets and how local cultures conferred both challenges and opportunities. More recently, the focus has shifted to comparative institutional approaches, in both helping explain the process of systemic development and change and enabling closer links to be drawn between HR practice and the wider political economy. This chapter locates the practice of HRM in Brunei within the wider political context, and draws out the implications for understanding continuity in change in HR practice, and similarities with and differences from other emerging markets.

One Emerging Market HR Paradigm or Many?

Cross-cultural approaches to HR have focused on the relative alignment of national cultural features and the specific defining features of HR practice. Although the literature on cross-cultural approaches is undeniably a diverse one, there are two broad common strands. The first is that common cultural features are shared across nations and regions, and the second is that many cultures in Africa and Asia share communitarian features (Horwitz & Budhwar, 2015). The latter, it has been argued, will support more mutually supportive modes of practice; the restraints imposed by formal policy and practice may be ameliorated by informal notions of mutuality and community (ibid.). Firms wishing to optimise outcomes should recognise, support, and sustain the latter.

Although this body of literature has been perfectly correct in pointing to the importance of culture, at the same time it has been open to three broad critiques. The first is that a focus on intangibles makes it very difficult to scientifically verify or disprove the very specific claims advanced as to national cultural characteristics around the world

(McSweeney, 2002). The second is that, as culture is very deeply embedded, it is difficult to explain systemic change, or indeed why the same basic culture can mutate to impart meaning in very different sets of circumstances (ibid.). Finally, cross-cultural approaches do not take account of the structure of and change in the global political economy, formal regulation, and relative resource endowments and allocations. In the case of Brunei, there is a shared culture and language with her two larger neighbours, but the country enjoys much larger per capita resource endowments and a distinct post-independence political evolution. Although culture can certainly explain some of the dynamics of business and HR in the context (see Hofstede, 2002), it will not be able to explain the latter.

In recent years, comparative institutional analysis has made strong headway in the international business and international and comparative HRM literatures. What sets such approaches apart is that an explicit linkage is drawn between the relative fortunes of nations and the nature of national-level institutional configurations. There are a number of different strands to this literature, but a key distinction is drawn between approaches based on 'property rights' and 'relationship' or socio-economic ones (Wood, Dibben, & Ogden, 2014; Brewster et al., 2015). The former takes a hierarchical view of institutions, in that a defining feature is simply how private property is protected, and, in turn, this moulds intra- and inter-organisational practice (Wood, Dibben, & Ogden, 2014; Brewster et al., 2015). In respect of HRM, it is held that in common law systems, owner rights are stronger than in civil law ones. In turn, this makes for weaker countervailing employee power (Wood, Dibben, & Ogden, 2014; Brewster et al., 2015). Hence, such systems are characterised by weaker security of tenure and more flexible labour markets, with firms having more room for manoeuvre in ejecting poor performers and replacing them with stronger performers secured in the external labour market (Gooderham et al., 2006). It is also held that common law perform better than civil law ones, although amongst the advanced societies the evidence is very mixed, and variations reflect the time period selected.

Brunei is, broadly speaking, a common law system, reflecting the English colonial tradition. However, the system is a hybrid one and also incorporates Islamic law, especially pertaining to family and property law (Mansurnoor, 2013). This means that there are a much greater range of restraints on social conduct, and indeed, on intra-workplace social relations; again, property rights in terms of general common law principles are mitigated by both Islamic law and the relative power of the Executive. Although this may dilute owner power, this does not make for a countervailing rise in worker power; rather, the position of both is relatively weak when compared to what might be encountered in mature institutional settings.

Convergence and Persistent Difference

In looking at emerging market institutions, there has been an increasing recognition that convergence with one or other of the mature market models is elusive; rather, national economies continue to develop on distinct lines, even if they are infused with some feature or another from one of the mature markets, most notably the liberal market economies (LMEs) (Wood, Dibben, & Ogden, 2014). In part this reflects an acceptance that national systems are not closely coupled (Lane & Wood, 2009). Even if, in objective terms, they are less than fully functional, they are likely to persist if they work well for insider interests and the latter have the will and the means to sustain their position (Wood & Frynas, 2005; Schneider, 2009).

Again, it can no longer be assumed that the mature varieties of capitalism represent islands of stability and balance. For example, the two largest LMEs, the US and the UK, have been associated with declining standards of living – and, indeed, working life – for a large proportion of the population, despite overall growth; the question is less whether systems work, but whether people have sufficient means to sustain themselves (O'Reilly et al., 2016). Whilst the US and the UK have now entered a period of open-ended political crisis, this reflects in part elite incompetence and bungling; it can be debated whether the latter reflects simply an elite overwhelmed by events, or senility on the part of an order unwilling or unable to sustain itself by conventional means (ibid.). In any case, no immediate fix or alternative is in sight. Again, if the LME model was previously sold as the gold standard for economic development, then its visible tarnishing means that it has become a less attractive model to be emulated.

This leads on to the question of whether there is more than one type of capitalism in emerging markets, or whether they are all similarly transitional. In the first decade of the 2000s, there were several attempts at developing national institutional archetypes to describe specific types of emerging market. Most notably, the concept of hierarchical market economies was developed to describe Latin America, segmented business systems for tropical Africa, family capitalism for selected Asian economies, and transitional peripheral economies for Central Asia (Wood & Frynas, 2005; Carney et al., 2009; Schneider, 2009; Demirbag et al., 2015). In each instance, these archetypes pointed to the internal segmentation between a relatively regulated state sector and large firms on the one hand, and weakly regulated small and informal employers on the other hand (ibid.). Again, informal extended networks of support compensate for failings in institutional coverage and support. Within the former, there is at least space for modern HR systems, and greater job and income security (ibid.). Medium and smaller firms are likely to be characterised by weak de facto legal regulation, and deeply embedded authoritarian managerial styles that may perpetuate great inequalities on gender, ethnic and income lines (ibid.). By the same measure, it may be mitigated by informal understandings of mutual obligation, with the informal provision of credit and leave in the cases of exceptional personal hardship (Webster et al., 2006). A high incidence of family ownership may impart further features, including a tendency to focus operations on where there is a family presence, and to seek opportunities for close collaboration with other businesses owned or controlled by family members (Chua et al., 2003; Madison et al., 2016). Again, there would be a preference for hiring family members, especially when it comes to managerial roles (ibid.).

Does this mean that there is only one variety of emerging market capitalism, rather than many, and that Brunei can easily be accommodated within this framework? Closer scrutiny would reveal that each of these taxonomies incorporates either explicitly or implicitly specific and deeply embedded historical features. For example, hierarchical market economies are partially what they are due to the long historical pattern of elite formation, and the extent to which in many Latin American countries, their patterns of behaviour have been persistently predatory (Schneider, 2009). Again, whilst embedded informal networks of support are widespread in emerging markets, in Central Asia they are clan-based, which makes them quite closed and impenetrable to outsiders (Demirbag et al., 2015). Finally, in Asia, many states have had far more room to pursue active industrial policies and more comprehensive infrastructural development initiatives than, say, their African counterparts (White, 2016); inter alia, this would reflect stronger traditions of state formation, and bargaining power in dealing with international financial institutions.

Where does this leave Brunei? Clearly it shares features with many other emerging markets. However, as noted above, it has a hybrid legal system, unlike many other former British colonies; this will impact on private property rights and, in turn, specific patterns of investor behaviour. The ultimate scale and scope of the ongoing trend towards a greater Islamification of the law imparts a further element of uncertainty (Croissant & Lorenz, 2018). Finally, recent work indicates that the English colonial legacy is a great deal more complex than commonly assumed; typically, colonial rule combined elements of constitutionalism with a security system vested with wide-ranging powers, and in many national contexts this has persisted into the postcolonial period (Wood et al., 2013). Brunei is no exception to this rule. Again, this means that both domestic and foreign economic agents have a loosely defined envelope of action; this necessitates a great deal of caution in dealing with a wide range of political and social matters, or, indeed, any activity that could be construed as straying into such domains (Croissant & Lorenz, 2018).

The Resource Curse and HRM

A further distinguishing feature of Brunei, which places it in a distinct category, is that it is a petro-state. Mellahi and Wood (2002) argue that such contexts typically constitute petroleum growth regimes. Such contexts are associated with specific institutional configurations, which are lopsided in that they are orientated primarily towards the resource sector, and which are often ineffective or, indeed, exert a negative influence, in sustaining other areas of the economy, with the exception of the state sector. Again, whilst institutions play a major role in ordering economic activities and sustaining growth, the great volatility of oil and gas prices makes it very difficult to smooth out the effects of any external shocks (Mellahi & Wood, 2002). In practice, this can lead to intervening periods of budgetary plenty and austerity; this means that the domain of active state involvement and support can rapidly expand and contract, with, in a downturn, areas deemed non-essential being readily jettisoned (cf. Croissant & Lorenz, 2018).

The extensive literature on the resource curse highlights the extent to which mineral booms are often associated with relative macroeconomic underperformance (Ross, 2015). Inter alia, natural resource windfalls lead to overvalued national currencies, the drain of skills and capital from non-mineral sectors, inefficiency and lavish patronage in the state sector, and ample opportunities for corruption (ibid.). Although petro-state governments often seek to diversify, their efforts often run into the sand in the face of these tendencies; in the end, national governments will tend to favour short-term solutions aimed at shoring up political stability, most commonly through further job creation in the state sector (ibid.; Badeep et al., 2017). Nor is the latter necessarily geared towards broadening the developmental basis of the state; the immediate aim is often to buy political stability through the extension of patronage to influential clans, tribes, or regions (Badeep et al., 2017). Brunei has faced all these pressures and tendencies. In practice, this has made for the trifurcation of HR practice. First, with the state sector, formal personnel administrative systems coexist with informal extended networks of support; invariably, the most influential of the latter will trump the former, leading to roles not necessarily being allocated on merit, arbitrary organisational growth in some divisions and stagnation in others, and personal authority and informal standing sometimes overriding formal position. Again, performance management is often ineffective, leading to great variations in productivity (Darwish et al., 2017).

Two other issues are worth reflecting on in terms of the relationship between the dominance of oil and gas in the national economy and the wider practice of HRM. First, a range of forces, ranging from the structural decline of oil and gas in the global energy mix, to the increasing importance of highly capital-intensive unconventional oil, has led to the petroleum industry becoming very financialised (Zhang et al., 2018). More specifically, there has been a move towards ever higher debt leverage, even to fund dividends. Although Brunei was built on conventional oil and gas, the proliferation of debt bubbles across the oil and gas industry means that any correction driven by declining demand (in the face of ever more competitive renewable sources), or even outright investor panic as the flood of cheap capital unleashed by quantitative easing dries up, may have a ricochet effect across the sector. In turn, this may lead to a rapid decline in reinvestment in oil and gas in Brunei, with unpredictable effects in terms of the sector's – and indeed, government's – ability to create and sustain jobs. Again, the rise of impact investors shunning oil and gas stocks – and, indeed, the increased caution of more conventional institutional investors towards them – has raised the spectre of 'stranded assets': investments in the oil and gas sector that are effectively unsaleable (Mercure et al., 2018). This may lead to even greater pressure on the Bruneian oil and gas industry, and indirectly, on the government jobs machine as well.

As with many other states with oil and gas windfalls, Brunei has a national Sovereign Wealth Fund (SWF); SWFs are intergenerational national savings devices, husbanding a proportion of foreign exchange windfalls for future generations. In practice, SWFs around the world vary greatly according to their relative transparency and their investment agendas; the latter may range from promoting more patient investment strategies to furthering national diplomatic efforts (Ahlashei, 2015). The Bruneian SWF, the 28th-ranked SWF in the world, still retains substantial assets despite a scandal involving the alleged misappropriation of significant funds (see Jetin & Chaisse, 2018). Recent research has indicated that proactive SWFs can make a significant impact on the HR strategies of target firms, even with shareholdings as little as 2%, for example by promoting a longer-term outlook and greater security of tenure (Goergen et al., 2018). Although there is little indication that Brunei's SWF has concerned itself with such issues, this would highlight the potential of the fund – and the country itself – to impact on HR around the world.

Expatriates and Local Labour

A further key issue is the role of expatriates. Although most of the literature on expatriates focuses on individuals who are highly skilled and paid, in many petro-states, ranging from the Gulf to Brunei, the bulk of expatriates are semi- and unskilled workers from relatively poor nations (Suphanchaimat et al., 2017; cf. Ullah & Kumpoh, 2019). This creates an additional segmentation within the labour market, with, in order of diminishing privilege, the indigenous elite; highly skilled, typically Western expatriates; the remaining indigenous workforce; and, most precarious all, unskilled and semi-skilled expatriates from other developing nations. The latter typically face deportation on loss of employment, enforcing labour compliance. At the same time, the large-scale usage of such workers brings with it risks, ranging from political stability – especially when such expatriates are from a much larger neighbouring state, such as Indonesia – to the risk of labour scandals, damaging the reputation of the country abroad (Suphanchaimat et al., 2017).

Conclusion

This chapter highlights the importance of viewing the development and nature of HR in Brunei from a long historical perspective. More particularly, specific colonial legacies and the resource boom have both created opportunities and challenges. Although natural resource revenues have provided for growth as well as providing the basis of national independence, they have also led to imbalances in the domestic economy, a drain on skills and capital to the oil and gas sector, and volatility. As the world enters a long energy transition, these contradictions are likely to be heightened. As with many petro-states, there is the challenge of both promoting other areas of industry and providing indigenous labour with skills and opportunities; however, both these challenges have proven extremely daunting, even in the case of the much larger Gulf petro-states. Looking forward, one possibility would be to shift the orientation of the national SWF to focus more directly on supporting an active industrial policy, although internal management issues in the fund would need resolving first. However, whatever the scale and scope of the country's developmental and HR challenges, these are very much less than those of a range of much poorer states within the region, and in relative terms the country remains a very attractive destination for a wide range of categories of labour.

Bibliography

Alhashel, B. (2015). Sovereign wealth funds: A literature review. *Journal of Economics and Business*, 78, 1–13.

Badeeb, R. A., Lean, H. H., & Clark, J. (2017). The evolution of the natural resource curse thesis: A critical literature survey. *Resources Policy*, 51, 123–134.

Brewster, C., Wood, G., & Goergen, M. (2015). Institutions, unionization and voice: The relative impact of context and actors on firm level practice. *Economic and Industrial Democracy*, 36, 2, 195–214.

Carney, M., Gedajlovic, E., & Yang, X. (2009). Varieties of Asian capitalism: Toward an institutional theory of Asian enterprise. *Asia Pacific Journal of Management*, 26, 3, 361–380.

Chua, J. H., Chrisman, J. J., & Sharma, P. (2003). Succession and nonsuccession concerns of family firms and agency relationship with nonfamily managers. *Family Business Review*, 16, 2, 89–107.

Croissant, A., & Lorenz, P. (2018). Brunei Darussalam: Malay Islamic monarchy and rentier state. In A. Croissant & P. Lorenz (eds), *Comparative politics of Southeast Asia*, 15–33. Cham: Springer.

Darwish, T. K., Mohamed, A. F., Wood, G., Singh, S., & Fleming, J. (2017). Can HRM alleviate the negative effects of the resource curse on firms? Evidence from Brunei. *Personnel Review*, 46, 8, 1931–1947.

Demirbag, M., McGuinness, M., Wood, G., & Bayyurt, N. (2015). Context, law and reinvestment decisions: Why the transitional periphery differs from other post-state socialist economies. *International Business Review*, 24, 6, 955–965.

Goergen, M., O'Sullivan, N., Wood, G., & Baric, M. (2018). Sovereign wealth funds, productivity and people: The impact of Norwegian Government Pension Fund-Global investments in the United Kingdom. *Human Resource Management Journal*, 28, 2, 288–303.

Gooderham, P., Nordhaug, O., & Ringdal, K., (2006). National embeddedness and calculative human resource management in US subsidiaries in Europe and Australia. *Human Relations*, 59, 11, 1491–1513.

Hofstede, G. (2002). Dimensions do not exist: A reply to Brendan McSweeney. *Human Relations*, 55, 11, 1355–1361.

Horwitz, F., & Budhwar, P. (2015). *Handbook of human resource management in emerging markets*. Cheltenham. Edward Elgar Publishing.

Jetin, B., & Chaisse, J. (2018). International investment policy for small states: The case of Brunei. In J. Chaisse & L. Nottage (eds), *International investment treaties and arbitration across Asia*, 384–410. Nijhoff: Brill.

Lane, C., & Wood, G. (2009). Capitalist diversity and diversity within capitalism. *Economy and Society*, 38, 4, 531–551.

Madison, K., Holt, D. T., Kellermanns, F. W., & Ranft, A. L. (2016). Viewing family firm behavior and governance through the lens of agency and stewardship theories. *Family Business Review*, 29, 1, 65–93.

Mansurnoor, I. (2013). Re-establishing order in Brunei: The introduction of the British legal system during the early residential period. *Islamic Studies*, 52, 2, 155–182.

McSweeney, B. (2002). Hofstede's model of national cultural differences and their consequences: A triumph of faith – a failure of analysis. *Human Relations*, 55, 1, 89–118.

Mellahi, K., & Wood, G. (2002). Desperately seeking stability: The making and remaking of the Saudi Arabian petroleum growth regime. *Competition and Change*, 6, 4, 345–362.

Mercure, J. F., Pollitt, H., Viñuales, J. E., Edwards, N. R., Holden, P. B., Chewpreecha, U., Salas, P., Sognnaes, I., Lam, A., & Knobloch, F. (2018). Macroeconomic impact of stranded fossil fuel assets. *Nature Climate Change*, 8, 7, 588.

O'Reilly, J., Froud, J., Johal, S., Williams, K., Warhurst, C., Morgan, G., Grey, C., Wood, G., Wright, M., Boyer, R., & Frerichs, S. (2016). Brexit: understanding the socio-economic origins and consequences. *Socio-Economic Review*, 14, 4, 807–854.

Ross, M. L. (2015). What have we learned about the resource curse? *Annual Review of Political Science*, 18, 239–259.

Schneider, B. R. (2009). Hierarchical market economies and varieties of capitalism in Latin America. *Journal of Latin American Studies*, 41, 3, 553–575.

Suphanchaimat, R., Pudpong, N., & Tangcharoensathien, V. (2017). Extreme exploitation in Southeast Asia waters: Challenges in progressing towards universal health coverage for migrant workers. *PLoS medicine*, 14, 11, p.e1002441.

Ullah, A. K. M., & Kumpoh, A. A. Z. (2019). Diaspora community in Brunei: Culture, ethnicity and integration. *Diaspora Studies*, 12, 1, 14–33.

Webster, E., Wood, G., & Brookes, M. (2006). International homogenization or the persistence of national practices? The remaking of industrial relations in Mozambique. *Relations Industrielles/Industrial Relations*, 61, 2, 247–270.

White, J. D. (2016). *The Chinese state in the era of economic reform: The road to crisis: Asia and the Pacific*. Abingdon: Routledge.

Wood, G., Brewster, C., & Brookes, M. (2014). *Human resource management and the institutional perspective*. Abingdon: Routledge.

Wood, G., Dibben, P., & Klerck, G. (2013). The limits of transnational solidarity: The congress of South African trade unions and the Swaziland and Zimbabwean crises. *Labor History*, 54, 5, 527–539.

Wood, G., Dibben, P., & Ogden, S. (2014). Comparative capitalism without capitalism, and production without workers: The limits and possibilities of contemporary institutional analysis. *International Journal of Management Reviews*, 16, 4, 384–396.

Wood, G., & Frynas, J. G. (2005). The institutional basis of economic failure: Anatomy of the segmented business system. *Socio-Economic Review*, 4, 2, 239–277.

Zhang, D., Wang, T., Shi, X., & Liu, J. (2018). Is hub-based pricing a better choice than oil indexation for natural gas? Evidence from a multiple bubble test. *Energy Economics*, 76, 495–503.

Contributors

Professor Geoffrey Wood is DanCap Chair of Innovation and Head of DAN Management at Western University in Canada, and Visiting Professor at Trinity College, Dublin. Previously, he served as Dean and Professor of International Business, at Essex Business School and before then as Professor of International Business at Warwick Business School, UK. He has authored/co-authored/edited eighteen books, and over one hundred and eighty articles in peer-reviewed journals. He also holds honorary positions at Griffith and Monash University in Australia, and Witwatersrand and Nelson Mandela Universities in South Africa. Geoffs research interests centre on the relationship between institutional setting, corporate governance, firm finance, and firm-level work and employment relations.

He is a Fellow of the Academy of Social Sciences, and a Fellow of the British Academy of Management, and is also in receipt of an Honorary Doctorate in economics from Aristotle University, Greece. Geoffrey Wood is Editor in Chief of the *British Journal of Management, Official Journal of the British Academy of Management* (BAM), and is Associate Editor of the *Academy of Management Perspectives, Official Journal of the Academy of Management* (US), as well as of *Human Resource Management*. He also serves at the BAM Council. He is also Co-Editor of the *Annals of Corporate Governance*. He is also editor of the Chartered ABS Journal Ranking list, and International Reviewer of the ABDC Journal Guide. He has had numerous research grants, including funding councils (e.g., ESRC), government departments (e.g., US Department of Labour; UK Department of Works and Pensions), charities (e.g., Nuffield Foundation), the labour movement (e.g., the ITF), and the European Union.

Professor Chris Brewster is Professor of International Human Resource Management at Henley Business School, University of Reading, in the UK. He had substantial experience as a practitioner and gained his doctorate from the LSE before becoming an academic. He researches in the field of international and comparative HRM, and he has published more than twenty-five books as well as over two hundred articles. He has taught in many countries around the world. In 2006, Chris was awarded an Honorary Doctorate by the University of Vaasa, Finland.

Dr Tamer K Darwish PhD, is a Reader in Human Resource Management (HRM) and the Head of HRM Research Centre in the Business School, University of Gloucestershire. He is also an Academic Fellow of the Chartered Institute of Personnel and Development. At Brunel University London, Tamer has received the Vice Chancellor's award for Research Excellence. His research interests lie in the areas of strategic HRM, international and comparative HRM, organizational performance, and knowledge management. He has published in these areas in leading management and HR journals including *Human Resource Management, British Journal of Management, European Management Review, Asia Pacific Journal of Management,* and the *International Journal of Human Resource Management.* He also serves on the editorial boards of a number of academic journals.

Mrs Jocelyne Fleming is a Senior Lecturer in the Business School at the University of Gloucestershire. Jocelyne has had a variety of management and leadership roles within the Public and Voluntary Sector. Her areas of teaching and research interests include leadership by design, change management, general management, strategy, and strategic human resource management.

Dr Washika Haak-Saheem holds a PhD in International Business Management from Leuphana University in Lüneburg, Germany. Prior to joining Henley Business School, she was an Associate Professor in Management and Human Resource Management at the University of Dubai in United Arab Emirates. At the University of Dubai, she was also the Programme Director of the undergraduate studies until July 2018. Before joining the academia in 2009, Washika worked in the airline industry in diverse roles and geographic locations for more than 12 years. Her recent research encompasses international human resource management, expatriation, global talent management, strategic human resource management, organizational behaviour in an international context, institutionalism, and knowledge management.

Her research on international HRM, expatriation, knowledge sharing appeared in journals such as *Human Resource Management Journal, International Journal of Human Resource Management, European Management Review,* and *International Journal of Cross Cultural Management.* She is a member of AIB, AOM, EGOS, EURAM, IFSAM, and SHRM. Washika is also an adjunct professor at the Hamburg School of Business Administration, where she delivers MBA and executive MBA in their global governance module.

Pengiran Muda Dr Abdul Fattaah Mohamed holds a BSc (Hons) degree in Business Economics and Computing, and an MA and PhD in International Management. He has worked in Brunei's Ministry of Foreign Affairs and has extensive experience in various aspects of international HR issues. He is currently the Chairman of Baiduri Bank, a leading bank in Brunei. He also holds directorships in a number of Bruneian companies. He regularly attends and delivers talks in academic and professional circles. His research interests lie in issues relating to international business, international HRM, and industrial relations. His research appeared in journals such as the *International Journal of Human Resource Management, Personnel Review*, and *Thunderbird International Business Review.*

Dr Satwinder Singh is Professor of International Business (IB) and Strategy at the University of Dubai, holds an MA (distinction) and PhD in Economics, and teaches IB- and Strategy-related subjects at postgraduate level. Previously, he has worked for the University of Reading (UK), Brunel University (UK), United Nations, and has conducted training programs in Africa and India. He is also an Associate Fellow at *The John H Dunning Centre for International Business*, University of Reading. An award-winning teacher, doctoral supervisor, and researcher he was awarded Brunel Business School staff award in 2013. He has published widely in the areas of IB, Strategy, and International Human Resource Management in reputed journals including *Human Resource Management, International Journal of Industrial Organization (IJIO), R&D Management, International Journal of HRM*, and *British Journal of Management*. He has also researched and published work in the area of entrepreneurship; his papers published in *IJIO* and the *African Journal of Economics and Management Studies* have respectively won 'Emerald Literati Network 2012 Outstanding Paper Award' and 'ANBAR Citation of Excellence Award'. Additionally, his paper Measuring Organizational Performance: A Case for Subjective Measures, *British Journal of Management*, Vol. 27, 214–224 (2016) was a top-cited paper for that year.

Index

Amable, B. 27
Anglo-Saxon world 27
Asian capitalisms 1, 96
autocratic-paternalist management 59
Auty, R. M. 52

Baiduri Bank 13
Bartlett, C. A. 41, 42, 121
benchmarking practices 28, 121
BIA *see* Brunei Investment
    Agency (BIA)
Birtch, T. 119
BLNG 12
Blunt, P. 125
board-level HR function 97
Bolkiah, Hassanal 8
Bonaccorsi, A. 63
Boschini, A. D. 60
Boxall, P. 17
Brewster, C. 17, 26, 110
British North Borneo Company 8
Brooke, James 8
Bruneian Labour Law 54, 56
Bruneian SWF 136
Brunei Darussalam 17–18, 52, 53–55,
    57, 58, 66, 67, 70, 75–77, 83, 89,
    104, 109, 118, 123–124, 126,
    132, 134–136; context and data
    96–97; economic profile 10–11;
    economy of 53, 78; geographic
    and demographic overview 7; high
    power–distance apparent in 125;
    historical overview of 7–9; HR in
    137; HRM in 14, 131; international
    affairs and organisations 9; legal
    system on 9; long-term development
    framework 15–17; net migration
    rate 78; non-oil and -gas sector
    industries 12–14; oil and gas
    industry 11–12

Brunei Empire 7
Brunei Investment Agency (BIA) 10
Brunei Methanol Company 14
Brunei Monetary Authority
    (AMBD) 13
Brunei Nationality Act (1961) 7
Brunei Shell Petroleum (BSP) 12
Bryane, M. 57
Budhwar, P. 17, 97
bureaucratic processes 16
business systems theory 64
Business Systems Theory 89, 90

capitalism: comparative 53, 58, 60; in
    emerging markets 133, 134
Carroll, S. J. 92
Chiang, F. 119
CMEs *see* coordinated market
    economies (CMEs)
Coff, R. W. 108
commodity-driven economies 76
Commons, John R. 92
communication 22, 30–31, 94,
    98, 119
commuters 40
comparative capitalism 53, 58, 60
comparative human resource
    management 3, 21–24, 26, 32, 45
comparative institutional analysis 64,
    90–92, 132
comparative literature 64
contextualising HRM 22
'contract manager' model 92
convergence: in HRM 28–32; and
    persistent difference 133–134
convergence-divergence debate 28
convergence theory 29
coordinated market economies
    (CMEs) 27
cross-cultural methods 59, 131–132

Cully, M. 107
cultural factors, HRM 25–28
cultural literature 22
cultural values 106

Darwish, T. 106
data 65–66
Debrah, Y. 17
De Cieri, H. 107
decision-making 126
De Guzman, G. M. 107
DEs *see* domestic enterprises (DEs)
discipline-related security 67
divergence, in HRM 28–32
Domestic and Multinational
  Enterprises 96
domestic enterprises (DEs) 1, 3–5,
  123, 126; in comparison to MNEs
  124; *vs.* MNEs 124–125
Doz, Y. L. 41

economic diversification 10, 14
Edwards, T. 113
Edwards, V. 110
emerging market capitalism 133, 134
empirical HRM studies 1–2
employee delegation 55
employees: recruitment of 105–106;
  recruitment, training, and retention
  of 104; retention practices of
  107–109; selection of 105–106;
  training practices of 106–107
European countries 32
European Union (EU) 28, 29; on
  human resource management 22
expatriates 136–137
extensive communication 30
extensive formal training 113

FDI *see* foreign direct
  investment (FDI)
Ferner, A. 106
Festing, M. 24
financial rewards 120
financial sector 12, 13
flexibility, in labour patterns 31
foreign direct investment (FDI) 17
foreign investment 83
foreign markets 41, 43, 107
frequent travellers 40
Frynas, J. G. 59
Fukuyama, F. 25
functional-level globalisation studies 37

GDP per capita 11, 14, 15
German MNEs 106
Germany, context of 107
Ghoshal, S. 41, 42, 121
globalisation 21, 22, 37, 40–41,
  121, 125
global mobility 39–40
Global Union Federations 54
GNP per capital 57
Gomez, E. T. 67
Guest, D. E. 38
Gulf Cooperation Council (GCC) 39
Gulf petro-states 137

Haak-Saheem, W. 24, 105, 110
Hall, P. A. 27
Harzing, A. W. 108
Hassan (1605–1619) 8
Hayden, A. 113
high-level HR practices 63
High Performance Work Systems
  (HPWSs) 80, 83
Hofstede, G. 43, 106, 125
Hollingsworth, J. R. 26
home country-based pressures 108
hospitality sector 13–14
HPWSs *see* High Performance Work
  Systems (HPWSs)
HR Directors 88–90, 97, 99, 109,
  123–124; role of 92–93, 95, 98
HRM *see* human resource
  management (HRM)
HR Manager 93
HRM practices *see* human resource
  management (HRM) practices
HR-related challenges 94
Hsu, Y. 105
Huang, T. 110
human resource culture 121–122
human resource development (HRD)
  15, 79–80, 82–84
human resource function 82, 88,
  89, 95, 97, 98; comparative
  development of 77
human resource (HR): in Brunei
  137; cross-cultural approaches to
  131–132; management of 82, 83
human resource (HR) practice 4, 5,
  52, 60–61, 66, 67, 75, 83, 89, 108,
  110, 113, 118, 120–122, 124–126,
  131, 135; HRM and organisational
  performance 80–82; implications
  for 98–99; individual effects of

68; institutional complementarity and 57–61; internal diversity at institutional level and 61–65; strategic value of 46; strategy, HR involvement and devolvement 79–80
human resource involvement 79–80
human resource management (HRM) 1, 131; convergence and divergence in 28–32; cultural and institutional factors 25–28; European model of 28; European Union on 22; importance in Brunei Darussalam 14; international dimension of 38–44; and organisational performance 80–82; outcomes measurement of 21; and resource curse 135–136
human resource management (HRM) functions 45, 85; role of 31–32
human resource management (HRM) policies 45
human resource management (HRM) practices 44, 104; interdependencies among 55–57; standardisation of 45
human resource policies 121; strategic value of 46
hypotheses 122–124

IB *see* international business (IB)
Ichniowski, C. 68
IFC *see* International Financial Centre (IFC)
IHRM *see* international human resource management (IHRM)
IJVs *see* international joint ventures (IJVs)
incentives 119–121, 126
indigenisation 55, 78, 82
industrial sector 14, 18
industries: company structure, objectives and strategies pursued by 95–96; non-oil and -gas sector 12–14
institutional complementarity, and HR practices 57–61
institutional factors, HRM 25–28
institutionalism 26, 27, 142
institutional literature 22
institutional redesign 65
interdependencies, among HRM practices 55–57

internal career opportunities: availability of 106; HRM practices 57
international affairs, in Brunei Darussalam 9
international business (IB) 37, 118, 132
International Financial Centre (IFC) 13
international human resource management (IHRM) 2, 3, 37, 38–39, 44–46, 97, 105, 118; country of origin 42; establishment method 42–43; globalisation 40–41; global mobility 39–40; organisational culture 43–44
internationalisation 41, 42
international joint ventures (IJVs) 37
international trade 37, 107
Islamic banking sector 13
Islamic Bank of Brunei Darussalam 13
Islamification 134

Jackson, S. E. 93
job-associated performance 125

knowledge-based economy (KBE) 16
Korea Gas Corporation 12
Kotey, B. 63

Labour Law enforcement 59
labour market regulation 69
labour markets 67, 69
Lake, D. 38
Leat, M. 105
legal system, on Brunei Darussalam 9
Lewis, M. 44
liberal market economies (LMEs) 27, 57, 58, 133
liberal markets 58
line management 30, 32, 80, 92
line managers 32, 75, 78–80, 92
literature: on comparative capitalism 27; developments of 58; on expatriates 136; institutional 22; on resource curse 135; review of 118
literature gaps 121
LMEs *see* liberal market economies (LMEs)
local labour 136–137
long-term development framework, Brunei Darussalam 15–17

McGaughey, S. L. 107
McMahan, G. C. 38
McPherson, A. H. 107
Magner, N. 108
managerial power, non-systematic
    practice of 69
marketing petro-state 75
Matlay, H. 108
maturity 14
Mellahi, K. 60, 135
micro-petro-state 75, 77
migrants 40, 78
mineral resource-rich 81
Ministry of Finance 10
MNEs *see* multinational enterprises
    (MNEs)
month-on-month-off 40
motivation theory 122
multinational enterprises (MNEs)
    1–5, 21, 37–43, 46, 88–90, 93–95,
    97–99, 104, 105, 108, 110–113,
    121, 123, 126; *vs.* DEs 124–125;
    development of 118; and local
    context 90–92; subsidiaries of
    44, 122

National Development Plan (NDP/
    RKN) 15, 54
negative relationship 81
net migration rate 78
non-financial rewards 119, 120
non-government organisations
    (NGOs) 39, 41
non-industrialised countries 18
non-oil and -gas sectors 12–14, 81; in
    petro-states 84
non-petroleum industries 10
non-resource-based industries 77, 91
non-resource-based sectors 53, 75, 76,
    81, 82
'norm entrepreneurship' 83, 88

oil and gas industry 1, 11–12, 96, 136
oil and gas sector 75, 81
Omar Ali, H. N. 13
OP *see* organisational
    performance (OP)
organisational competitiveness 76–77
organisational culture 43–44
organisational performance (OP)
    80–82
organisational strategy 88
organisation-focused skills 63

organisations 40, 41, 55, 61, 64,
    65, 80, 97; in Brunei Darussalam
    9; principles of 23–24; in United
    Kingdom 106
Osaka Gas Company 12
Outline of Strategies and Policies for
    Development (OSPD) 15, 53–54

Partai Rakyat Brunei 8
part-time working 31
PAs *see* performance appraisals (PAs)
paternalism 65
performance appraisals (PAs) 119,
    122, 124–126
performance-based rewards 108
performance management 135
petro-state governments 77
petro-states 62, 69, 70, 75, 82; non-oil
    and -gas sectors in 84
Pfeffer, J. 23, 24
positive relationship 81
Prahalad, C. K. 41
Privatisation Master Plan 17
public ownership 26
Pulau Muara Besar (PMB) industrial
    site 14

'Rakyat Melayu' 15
rationalisation 57, 67
recruitment: of employees 105–106;
    HRM practices 56
Redding, G. 96
Reiche, B. S. 107
resource curse 53, 63, 75, 84; and
    HRM 135–136; literature 81; and
    organisational competitiveness 76–77
Resource Curse Theory 69
retention practices, of employees
    107–109
rewards 119–121, 126
Roche, W. K. 107
Rowley, C. 44
Royal Dutch/Shell group 12

Sagiv, L. 25
Sawyer, S. 67
Scholte, J. A. 41
Schuler, R. S. 93
Schwartz, S. H. 25
segmented business systems 59
selection: of employees 105–106;
    HRM practices 56
self-initiated expatriates 40

semi-skilled employees 77
Seri Begawan 8–9
Sharia law 9
Shaw, J. D. 108
Shaw, K. 68
Shen, J. 110
Sheridan, A. 63
short-term expatriates 40
SHRM *see* strategic human resource management (SHRM)
Singh, S. 93, 99, 106, 124
skills-based rewards 120
small- to medium-sized enterprises (SMEs) 14, 37
Snell, S. A. 38
Sorge, A. 108
Soskice, D. 27
South China Sea 7
Sovereign Wealth Fund (SWF) 136
standardisation 44–45, 95; of HRM practices 45
strategic decision-making 79, 88
strategic HR devolvement (SHRD) 75, 76, 81
strategic HR involvement (SHRI) 75, 76, 81, 83
strategic human resource management (SHRM) 21, 23, 24, 38, 90, 112
Sultan Omar Ali Saifuddien III 8
SWF *see* Sovereign Wealth Fund (SWF)
Szamosi, L. T. 108

talent management 112
Tanova, C. 64
Tan, S. E. 13
Tasie, G. 18
temporary employment 31
Todaro, M. 40–41
Tokyo Electric Power Company (TEPCO) 12
Tokyo Gas Company 12

top-down method 62
Trade Union Act (1961) 54
trade union membership 30
training practices: of employees 106–107; HRM practices 56–57
Trans-Pacific Strategic Economic Agreement 9
two-way communication 126
Type B HR Directors 93
Tyson, S. 92

Ulrich, D. 38
UNDP human development index 11, 57
United Kingdom (UK) 133; organisations in 106; training initiatives in 107
United Nations (UN) 39
United States (US) 133
universalist paradigm 21, 23
unskilled employees 77
upward communication 30
US-based HR concepts 22
US model of HRM 30

Vaiman, V. 26
value-added HR models 80–81
value-added HR practices 61, 63–65, 67
values 44; defined as 43
Verburg, R. M. 106
Von Glinow, M. A. 106

'Wawasan Brunei 2035' 15, 53
Westernisation 41
Western MNEs 110
Whitley, R. 55–56
Witt, M. A. 96
Wood, G. 26, 59, 60, 135
World Bank Doing Business Reports 69
Wright, P. M. 38

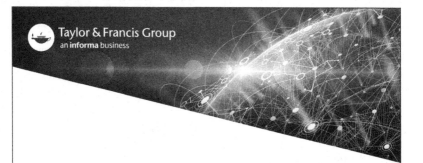

Printed in the United States
by Baker & Taylor Publisher Services